TEACHER'S PET PUBLICATIONS

LITPLAN TEACHER PACK
for
Inherit the Wind
based on the play by
Jerome Lawrence & Robert E. Lee

Written by
Mary B. Collins

© 1996 Teacher's Pet Publications
All Rights Reserved

This **LitPlan** for Lawrence and Lee's
Inherit the Wind
has been brought to you by Teacher's Pet Publications, Inc.

Copyright Teacher's Pet Publications 1996
11504 Hammock Point
Berlin MD 21811

Only the student materials in this unit plan (such as worksheets,
study questions, and tests) may be reproduced multiple times
for use in the purchaser's classroom.

For any additional copyright questions,
contact Teacher's Pet Publications.

www.tpet.com

TABLE OF CONTENTS - *Inherit the Wind*

Introduction	5
Unit Objectives	7
Reading Assignment Sheet	8
Unit Outline	9
Study Questions (Short Answer)	13
Quiz/Study Questions (Multiple Choice)	18
Pre-reading Vocabulary Worksheets	29
Lesson One (Introductory Lesson)	39
Nonfiction Assignment Sheet	40
Oral Reading Evaluation Form	43
Writing Assignment 1	41
Writing Assignment 2	42
Writing Assignment 3	60
Writing Evaluation Form	61
Vocabulary Review Activities	49
Extra Writing Assignments/Discussion ?s	47
Unit Review Activities	62
Unit Tests	65
Unit Resource Materials	93
Vocabulary Resource Materials	107

A FEW NOTES ABOUT THE AUTHORS
Lawrence and Lee

Jerome Lawrence was born on July 14, 1915 in Cleveland, Ohio. He graduated from Ohio State University with a B. A. degree in 1937 and completed his graduate study at the University of California, Los Angeles in 1939. He began his career as a reporter and telegraph editor for the *Wilmington News Journal* in Wilmington, Ohio. The most noteworthy event in his early career was his chance meeting with Robert E. Lee in a restaurant in New York City in 1942. The two men subsequently formed a partnership which proved to be long-lasting, productive, and very successful.

Robert E. Lee was born in Elyria, Ohio on October 14, 1918. He attended Northwestern University, Ohio Wesleyan University, Western Reserve University, and Drake University. In 1948 he married Janet Waldo, and they had two children, a boy and a girl.

Together, Lawrence and Lee not only wrote the powerful play *Inherit the Wind*, but also wrote such famous works as *Auntie Mame, Only in America, Mame, Dear World, The Night Thoreau Spent in Jail, The Incomparable Max!, The Crocodile Smile, and Jabberwock* . . . . Their other accomplishments range from being the founders of the Armed Forces Radio Service to writing, directing, and/or producing other many other plays as well as radio and television programs including "Hollywood Showcase," "I Was There," "Orson Welles Theatre," "Frank Sinatra Show," "Hallmark Hall of Fame," "Times Square Playhouse," and "Lincoln: The Unwilling Warrior."

The list of awards these two authors have won, the list of their achievements, and the list of the work they have done in their careers is as long as a child's list for Santa Claus.

INTRODUCTION

This unit has been designed to develop students' reading, writing, thinking, and language skills through exercises and activities related to *Inherit the Wind* by Lawrence and Lee. It includes eighteen lessons, supported by extra resource materials.

The **introductory lesson** introduces students to the novel through a writing assignment. Following the introductory activity, students are given a transition to explain how the activity relates to the book they are about to read. Following the transition, students are given the materials they will be using during the unit. At the end of the lesson, students begin the pre-reading work for the first reading assignment.

The **reading assignments** are approximately thirty pages each; some are a little shorter while others are a little longer. Students have approximately 15 minutes of pre-reading work to do prior to each reading assignment. This pre-reading work involves reviewing the study questions for the assignment and doing some vocabulary work for 8 to 10 vocabulary words they will encounter in their reading.

The **study guide questions** are fact-based questions; students can find the answers to these questions right in the text. These questions come in two formats: short answer or multiple choice. The best use of these materials is probably to use the short answer version of the questions as study guides for students (since answers will be more complete), and to use the multiple choice version for occasional quizzes. If your school has the appropriate equipment, it might be a good idea to make transparencies of your answer keys for the overhead projector.

The **vocabulary work** is intended to enrich students' vocabularies as well as to aid in the students' understanding of the book. Prior to each reading assignment, students will complete a two-part worksheet for approximately 8 to 10 vocabulary words in the upcoming reading assignment. Part I focuses on students' use of general knowledge and contextual clues by giving the sentence in which the word appears in the text. Students are then to write down what they think the words mean based on the words' usage. Part II nails down the definitions of the words by giving students dictionary definitions of the words and having students match the words to the correct definitions based on the words' contextual usage. Students should then have an understanding of the words when they meet them in the text.

After each reading assignment, students will go back and formulate answers for the study guide questions. Discussion of these questions serves as a **review** of the most important events and ideas presented in the reading assignments.

After students complete reading the work, there is a **vocabulary review** lesson which pulls together all of the fragmented vocabulary lists for the reading assignments and gives students a review of all of the words they have studied.

A lesson is devoted to the **extra discussion questions/writing assignments**. These questions focus on interpretation, critical analysis and personal response, employing a variety of thinking skills and adding to the students' understanding of the novel.

There is one **group activity** in which students work in small groups to discuss issues related to *Inherit the Wind*.

The group activity is followed by a **reports and discussion** session in which the groups share their ideas about the themes with the entire class; thus, the entire class is exposed to information about all of the themes and the entire class can discuss each theme based on the nucleus of information brought forth by each of the groups.

There are three **writing assignments** in this unit, each with the purpose of informing, persuading, or having students express personal opinions. The first assignment is to express personal opinions: students give their own views on how mankind came to exist. The second assignment is to inform: students write a summary of the nonfiction articles they have read in preparation for an oral presentation. The third assignment is to persuade: students write an persuasive essay regarding whether or not Darwin's theories will become totally accepted as Menken predicted.

In addition, there is a **nonfiction reading assignment**. Students are required to read a piece of nonfiction related in some way to *Inherit the Wind*. After reading their nonfiction pieces, students will fill out a worksheet on which they answer questions regarding facts, interpretation, criticism, and personal opinions. During one class period, students make **oral presentations** about the nonfiction pieces they have read. This not only exposes all students to a wealth of information, it also gives students the opportunity to practice **public speaking**.

The **review lesson** pulls together all of the aspects of the unit. The teacher is given four or five choices of activities or games to use which all serve the same basic function of reviewing all of the information presented in the unit.

The **unit test** comes in two formats: multiple choice or short answer. As a convenience, two different tests for each format have been included. There is also an advanced short answer test for students who need more of a challenge.

There are additional **support materials** included with this unit. The **extra activities** section includes suggestions for an in-class library, crossword and word search puzzles related to the novel, and extra vocabulary worksheets. There is a list of **bulletin board ideas** which gives the teacher suggestions for bulletin boards to go along with this unit. In addition, there is a list of **extra class activities** the teacher could choose from to enhance the unit or as a substitution for an exercise the teacher might feel is inappropriate for his/her class. **Answer keys** are located directly after the **reproducible student materials** throughout the unit. The student materials may be reproduced for use in the teacher's classroom without infringement of copyrights. No other portion of this unit may be reproduced without the written consent of Teacher's Pet Publications, Inc.

UNIT OBJECTIVES - *Inherit the Wind*

1. Through reading *Inherit the Wind* students will gain a better understanding of the issue of creation versus evolution.

2. Students will demonstrate their understanding of the text on four levels: factual, interpretive, critical and personal.

3. Students will consider recent issues and problems concerned with determining what will be taught in public schools.

4. Students will be given the opportunity to practice reading aloud and silently to improve their skills in each area.

5. Students will answer questions to demonstrate their knowledge and understanding of the main events and characters in *Inherit the Wind* as they relate to the author's theme development.

6. Students will enrich their vocabularies and improve their understanding of the novel through the vocabulary lessons prepared for use in conjunction with the novel.

7. The writing assignments in this unit are geared to several purposes:
    a. To have students demonstrate their abilities to inform, to persuade, or to express their own personal ideas
        NOTE: Students will demonstrate ability to write effectively to <u>inform</u> by developing and organizing facts to convey information. Students will demonstrate the ability to write effectively to <u>persuade</u> by selecting and organizing relevant information, establishing an argumentative purpose, and by designing an appropriate strategy for an identified audience. Students will demonstrate the ability to write effectively to <u>express personal ideas</u> by selecting a form and its appropriate elements.
    b. To check the students' reading comprehension
    c. To make students think about the ideas presented by the novel
    d. To encourage logical thinking
    e. To provide an opportunity to practice good grammar and improve students' use of the English language.

8. Students will read aloud, report, and participate in large and small group discussions to improve their public speaking and personal interaction skills.

READING ASSIGNMENTS - *Inherit the Wind*

Date Assigned	Assignment	Completion Date
	Act 1 Scene 1	
	Act 1 Scene 2, Act 2 Scene 1	
	Act 2 Scene 2	
	Act 3	

NOTES: Since *Inherit the Wind* is a play, it is really meant to be acted out on the stage. If you and your students are so inclined and interested, a production with minimal props is possible. This unit is not planned for a complete production. However, it is planned to have the parts spoken by various students during in-class reading. A list of characters needed for reading in each class period is provided. Try to arrange your assignments of parts so that each student will have an opportunity to "play" a part at least once.

UNIT OUTLINE - *Inherit the Wind*

1 Introduction	2 Assign Parts Practice Reading	3 Read 1:1	4 Read 1:2 Study ?s Act 1 PV Act 2	5 Read 2:1 & 2:2
6 Finish 2:2 Study ?s Act 2 PV Act 3	7 Read Act 3	8 Study ?s Act 3 Extra ?s	9 Vocabulary	10 Library
11 Reading & Sm. Group Discussion	12 Writing Assignment #2	13 Reports & Class Discussion	14 Scopes Trial	15 Scopes Trial
16 Writing Assignment #3	17 Review	18 Test		

Key: P=Preview Study Questions   V=Prereading Vocabulary Worksheet

STUDY GUIDE QUESTIONS

SHORT ANSWER STUDY GUIDE QUESTIONS - *Inherit the Wind*

Act One
1. What does Howard call Melinda and her whole family?
2. Why did Rachael go to the courthouse?
3. Why was Bert Cates in jail?
4. What did Darwin's *Origin* say?
5. Why did Rev. Brown want the sign put up?
6. Who is E. K. Hornbeck?
7. What kind of a man does E. K. Hornbeck appear to be?
8. Who is Matthew Harrison Brady?
9. How does Brady want the Mayor and Reverend to look for the picture?
10. How does Mrs. Brady treat Mr. Brady?
11. Who is the Baltimore *Herald* sending to Hillsboro (besides E. K. Hornbeck)?
12. What does Drummond accomplish on the first day of the trial?
13. What explanation does Drummond give Bert as to why people look at him "worse than a murderer"?
14. What warning does Bert give Rachael?

Act Two
1. What does Rev. Brown pray for when Rachael asks him not to damn Bert?
2. What is Brady's reaction to Brown's damnation of his own daughter?
3. What does Drummond try to establish when questioning Howard?
4. For what reason is Bert on trial, according to Drummond?
5. What did Rev. Brown say about Tommy Stebbins?
6. Why did Bert leave the church?
7. What "humorous" remark had Bert made about the Heavenly Father?
8. What problem did Drummond have with his expert witnesses?
9. As a last resort, who does Drummond call to the witness stand? Why?
10. What does Drummond gain by questioning the belief in the literal translation of the Bible?
11. Why did Drummond want Brady to admit that the first day could have been 25 hours long?
12. Who is the Prophet from Nebraska?
13. What does Brady do at the end of his testimony?

Act Three
1. Identify Golden Dancer.
2. What was the jury's verdict?
3. What was Bert's sentence?
4. What happened to Brady?
5. Did Bert win or lose?
6. Who paid bail for Bert?
7. What decision has Rachael made?
8. To what does Rachael compare ideas?
9. Drummond says Brady had the same right as Cates. What right is that?
10. How will Cates' case be appealed?

ANSWER KEY: SHORT ANSWER STUDY GUIDE QUESTIONS - *Inherit the Wind*

<u>Act One</u>

1. What does Howard call Melinda and her whole family?
    He calls them worms.

2. Why did Rachael go to the courthouse?
    She went to see Bert Cates in jail.

3. Why was Bert Cates in jail?
    He read Darwin's *Origin of the Species* to his class.

4. What did Darwin's *Origin* say?
    It said that "man wasn't just stuck here like a geranium in a flower pot; that living comes from a long miracle, it just didn't happen in seven days."

5. Why did Rev. Brown want the sign put up?
    He wanted to show Mr. Brady "at once what kind of a community this is."

6. Who is E. K. Hornbeck?
    He is a reporter from the Baltimore *Herald*. He has come to cover Bert Cates' trial.

7. What kind of a man does E. K. Hornbeck appear to be?
    He is independent, not very friendly, and downright insulting to many citizens. He has a sarcastic wit which, although offensive, shows insight and intelligence.

8. Who is Matthew Harrison Brady?
    He is the attorney prosecuting Bert Cates' case. He has come to Hillsboro for the trial. Also, he has been a Presidential candidate and is obviously a politician who gives great speeches and gathers many followers.

9. How does Brady want the Mayor and Reverend to look for the picture?
    He wants them to look "hopeful."

10. How does Mrs. Brady treat Mr. Brady?
    She mothers him.

11. Who is the Baltimore *Herald* sending to Hillsboro (besides E. K. Hornbeck)?
    They are sending Henry Drummond, a lawyer who "has stalked courtrooms of this land for forty years. When he fights, headlines follow."

12. What does Drummond accomplish on the first day of the trial?
    He attempts to get impartial jurors and points out some obvious inequities in the situation. One goal seems to be to upset Brady and shake things up a bit to lessen the prosecution's grasp on the case. He objects to Brady's title of Colonel and to the Read Your Bible banner, for example.

13. What explanation does Drummond give Bert as to why people look at him "worse than a murderer"?
    "You murder a wife, it isn't nearly as bad as murdering an old wives' tale."

14. What warning does Bert give Rachael?
    If she repeats things he has talked about to her in confidence, he is sure he will be convicted.

Act Two

1. What does Rev. Brown pray for when Rachael asks him not to damn Bert?
   He calls "down the same curse on those who ask grace for this sinner."

2. What is Brady's reaction to Brown's damnation of his own daughter?
   ". . . it is possible to be overzealous, to destroy that which you hope to save--so that nothing is left but emptiness. Remember the wisdom of Solomon in the Book of Proverbs--He that troubleth his own house. . . shall inherit the wind."

3. What does Drummond try to establish when questioning Howard?
   ". . . that Howard--or Col. Brady--or Charles Darwin--or anyone in this courtroom--or *you*, sir-- has the right to *think*."

4. For what reason is Bert on trial, according to Drummond?
   ". . . he is threatened with fine and imprisonment because he chooses to speak what he thinks."

5. What did Rev. Brown say about Tommy Stebbins?
   He said that Tommy's soul was damned, writhing in hellfire, because Tommy died before his parents had him baptized.

6. Why did Bert leave the church?
   After Rev. Brown's preaching about Tommy Stebbins, Bert left because he believed religion was "to comfort people, not frighten them to death."

7. What "humorous" remark had Bert made about the Heavenly Father?
   He had said, "God created Man in His own image--and Man, being a gentleman, returned the compliment."

8. What problem did Drummond have with his expert witnesses?
> The judge ruled that their testimony was not relevant to the case, and he refused to allow them to be questioned.

9. As a last resort, who does Drummond call to the witness stand? Why?
> He calls Brady to the stand to deliver testimony about the Bible since that seems to be the only thing admissible.

10. What does Drummond gain by questioning the belief in the literal translation of the Bible?
> He gets Brady to say that the only explanation is that if the Lord wishes it, it can be so. This leads to the almost ridiculous comparison between a man's being granted the same privilege (of thinking) that a sponge has.

11. Why did Drummond want Brady to admit that the first day could have been 25 hours long?
> It would (and did) open the way for the conclusion that the day could have been any length of time--even millions of years.

12. Who is the Prophet from Nebraska?
> That is what Drummond called Brady after Brady said that God speaks to him and he acts accordingly.

13. What does Brady do at the end of his testimony?
> He begins to chant the books of the Bible.

Act Three

1. Identify Golden Dancer.
> Golden Dancer was a rocking horse that Drummond wanted as a child. It looked great in the store window, but when he finally got it, it was rotten and fell apart.

2. What was the jury's verdict?
> They found Bert Cates guilty.

3. What was Bert's sentence?
> He had to pay a $100.00 fine.

4. What happened to Brady?
> He died.

5. Did Bert win or lose?
> Because his sentence was so light, he won even though he was found guilty.

6. Who paid bail for Bert?
> The Baltimore *Herald* paid the bail money.

7. What decision has Rachael made?
   She decided to leave her father and go out on her own.

8. To what does Rachael compare ideas?
   She compares them to children inside our bodies; they have to be born, to come out. The good ones will live and the sickly ones will mostly die.

9. Drummond says Brady had the same right as Cates. What right is that?
   They both have the right to be wrong.

10. How will Cates' case be appealed?
    Drummond implied he would do it for free.

MULTIPLE CHOICE STUDY GUIDE/QUIZ QUESTIONS - *Inherit the Wind*

Act One

1. What does Howard call Melinda and her whole family?
    A. He calls them monkeys.
    B. He calls them worms.
    C. He calls them imbeciles.
    D. He calls them heathens and pagans.

2. Why did Rachel go to the courthouse?
    A. She went to see Bert Cates in jail.
    B. She went to get a good seat for the trial.
    C. She went to talk to the judge.
    D. She went to take lunch to the warden.

3. Bert Cates was in jail because he read a book to his class. What was the book?
    A. He had read *The Communist Manifesto* by Marx.
    B. He had read the writings of Confucius.
    C. He had read Darwin's *Origin of the Species.*
    D. He had read Freud's *Interpretation of Dreams.*

4. True or False: The text said that "man wasn't just stuck here like a geranium in a flower pot; that living comes from a long miracle; it didn't just happen in seven days."
    A. True
    B. False

5. Why did the Reverend Brown want the sign put up?
    A. He wanted to show Mr. Brady what kind of community they had.
    B. He wanted to advertise to get visitors to attend his Sunday services. He'd get more in the collection plate that way.
    C. He was hoping to attract media attention.
    D. He didn't want to hurt the feelings of the women who had spent so long making it.

6. Who is E. K. Hornbeck?
    A. He is the state superintendent of schools.
    B. He is the head of the Science Department at the University of North Carolina.
    C. He is a movie director from Hollywood.
    D. He is a reporter for the Baltimore *Herald* newspaper.

7. True or False: E. K. Hornbeck is independent but amiable. He has a way with people and gets them to open up easily. He is quick-witted and makes insightful yet friendly jokes.
    A. True
    B. False

Inherit the Wind Multiple Choice Study Questions Page 2

8. Which of the following does not describe Matthew Harrison Brady?
    A. He is the attorney prosecuting the case.
    B. He is a former Presidential candidate.
    C. He is a professor at the Harvard School of Law.
    D. He is a famous speaker with a large following.

9. How does Brady want the Mayor and Reverend to look for the picture?
    A. He wants them to look pious.
    B. He wants them to look serious and intelligent.
    C. He wants them to look angry and righteous.
    D. He wants them to look hopeful.

10. How does Mrs. Brady treat Mr. Brady?
    A. She mothers him.
    B. She ignores him.
    C. She is polite but not loving.
    D. She is obviously afraid of him and does whatever he says.

11. Who is Henry Drummond?
    A. He is the head of the American Civil Liberties Union. He has been sent to follow the trial.
    B. He is the prelate of the Church of Christ Scientist. He is coming to testify for Cates.
    C. He is a well-known lawyer who has been sent by the Baltimore *Herald* to defend Cates.
    D. He is a senator who is up for re-election. He is supporting the town's side of the argument because he thinks it will get him more votes.

12. Drummond accomplishes many things on the first day of the trial. Which of these is not one of them?
    A. He attempts to get impartial jurors.
    B. He shakes things up to lessen Brady's hold on the case.
    C. He objects to Brady's title of Colonel and the Read Your Bible banner.
    D. He organizes a support group for Cates.

13. True or False: Drummond tells Bert Cates that people look at him as "worse than a murderer" because defaming the Bible is worse than any crime against people.
    A. True
    B. False

Inherit the Wind Multiple Choice Study Questions Page 3

14. What warning does Bert give Rachel?
    A. He tells her that she will be ostracized if she associates with him.
    B. He tells her that she should leave town and go to a large northern city that has a more liberal attitude.
    C. He tells her that Brady is out to get her, too.
    D. He tells her that if she repeats things he has talked about to her in confidence, he is sure he will be convicted.

Inherit the Wind Multiple Choice Study Questions Page 4

Act Two

15. What does Reverend Brown pray for when Rachael asks him not to damn Bert?
    A. He calls down "the same curse on those who ask grace for this sinner."
    B. He prays for "the wisdom and grace to see the Lord's holy plan."
    C. He prays for "the demons of evil to flee from this innocent child"
    D. He calls down "the avenging angels to lift the sinners and carry them away from temptation."

16. Brady reacts to Reverend Brown's comments by repeating the following quote: "...it is possible to be overzealous, to destroy that which you hope to save--so that nothing is left but emptiness. Remember ..'He that troubleth his own house...shall inherit the wind.'" Where does this quote come from?
    A. Ironically, it comes from *The Origin of the Species*. Brady had read it in a magazine article and jotted it down, but he didn't remember the original source.
    B. It comes from Brady's acceptance speech for the Presidency--the speech he never had the chance to give.
    C. It comes from the Book of Proverbs.
    D. It comes from the writings of Thomas Jefferson.

17. True or False: While questioning Howard, Drummond tries to establish that everyone has the right to think.
    A. True
    B. False

18. For what reason is Bert on trial, according to Drummond?
    A. He is on trial for corrupting the morals of minors.
    B. He is on trial for choosing to speak what he thinks.
    C. He is on trial for destroying the religious beliefs of the community.
    D. He is on trial for willfully disobeying the School Board.

19. What did Reverend Brown say about Tommy Stebbins's unbaptized soul?
    A. He said Tommy's soul would automatically go the Heaven.
    B. He said Tommy's soul would stay in Purgatory until the time of the Second Coming of Christ.
    C. He said Tommy's soul would be condemned to hellfire forever.
    D. He said there was a chance that Tommy's soul could be saved if his parents would repent, become re-baptized, and work as missionaries for the rest of their lives.

Inherit the Wind Multiple Choice Study Questions Page 5

20. Why did Bert leave the church?
    A. His two hours of supervised parole were expired.
    B. He disagreed with the Reverend Brown's sermon.
    C. He had a secret meeting arranged with Rachel. It was a good time to meet since most of the townspeople, including her father, were busy.
    D. He believed that "The Lord helps those who help themselves". He went to prepare his case.

21. Finish Bert's "Humorous" comment about the Heavenly Father. "God created Man in His own image..."
    A. "...and God had a poor imagination."
    B. "...and it was the only mistake He ever made."
    C. "..then He made lawyers to straighten things out."
    D. "...man, being a gentleman, returned the compliment."

22. What problem did Drummond have with his expert witnesses?
    A. None of them showed up. They had been secretly detoured to another town by cohorts of the Reverend Brown and could not get transportation to the trial.
    B. The judge ruled that their testimony was not relevant to the case, and he refused to allow them to be questioned.
    C. They were afraid to testify because they had received threats.
    D. The newspaper, which was paying them, collapsed under pressure from its directors and withdrew their financial support. None of the witnesses would appear for free.

23. As a last resort, who does Drummond call to the stand?
    A. He calls. Reverend Brown to the stand.
    B. He calls E. K. Hornbeck to the stand.
    C. He calls Brady to the stand.
    D. He calls himself to the stand.

24. True or False: By questioning the literal translation of the Bible,(if the Lord wishes it, it can be so), Drummond arrives at the conclusion that a man has the same privilege of thinking as a sponge has.
    A. True
    B. False

25. True or False: Drummond wanted Brady to admit that the first day could have been 25 hours long to show how ridiculous Brady's thinking was.
    A. True
    B. False

Inherit the Wind Multiple Choice Study Questions Page 6

26. What does Drummond call Brady after Brady says that God speaks to him and he acts accordingly?
    A. He calls Brady "God's Other Son."..
    B. He calls Brady "Your Holiness."
    C. He calls Brady the "Prophet from Nebraska."
    D. He calls Brady "Colonel Matthew the Archangel."

27. What does Brady do at the end of his testimony?
    A. He sings "Rock of Ages."
    B. He begins to chant the books of the Bible.
    C. He calls for Holy Water to wash away the demons.
    D. He cries and calls for his wife.

Inherit the Wind Multiple Choice Study Questions Page 7

Act Three

28. Identify Golden Dancer.
    A. It was a nickname given to Rachel when she was little. She wanted to be a dancer and was showing talent. He father forbade her from continuing because he said it was sinful.
    B. It was a rocking horse that Drummond wanted as a child. It looked great in the store window, but when he finally got it, it was rotten and fell apart.
    C. It was the title of a book Bert Cates had read when he was younger. It was the book that started him thinking about freedom of speech.
    D. It was a code name E. K. Hornbeck was using to secretly telegraph information about the trial to his editor.

29. What was the jury's verdict?
    A. They found Bert Cates guilty.
    B. They found Bert Cates not guilty.
    C. It was a hung jury.
    D. Bert got off on a technicality.

30. What happened to Bert?
    A. He had to do community service for a year.
    B. He was asked to leave town by the end of the week.
    C. He had to undergo a psychiatric evaluation.
    D. He had to pay a $100.00 fine.

31. What happened to Brady?
    A. He collapsed and died.
    B. He went home to his farm and never again appeared in public.
    C. He went to divinity school.
    D. He vowed to take the case to the Supreme Court.

32. Did Bert win or lose?
    A. He won. Even though he was found guilty, his sentence was very light.
    B. He lost. His future in the town is ruined..
    C. He won but felt bad about doing so.
    D. He lost because his wife left him.

33. Who paid bail for Bert?
    A. Rachael paid it.
    B. The Baltimore *Herald* paid it.
    C. Drummond paid it.
    D. Cates paid it himself.

Inherit the Wind Multiple Choice Study Questions Page 8

34. What decision has Rachael made?
    A. She is going to marry Bert.
    B. She is going to teach in Bert's place and continue his work.
    C. She is going to study anthropology.
    D. She is going to leave her father and go out on her own.

35. To what does Rachael compare ideas?
    A. She compares them to children inside our bodies; they have to be born, to come out. The good ones will live and the sickly ones will mostly die.
    B. She compares them to rivers. Some grow deep and wide while others slow to a trickle.
    C. She compares them to anthills. Even if they get stepped on, they can be built back up.
    D. She compares them to the moon. They may be fully or partially developed, but they will always be there, tugging at us.

36. Drummond says Brady had the same right as Cates. What right is that?
    A. It is the right to be wrong.
    B. It is the right to live as he believes.
    C. It is the right to appeal the case.
    D. It is the right to privacy after the trial's conclusion.

37. How will Cates's case be appealed?
    A. The students have collected enough money to pay for it.
    B. Rachael has donated her life savings to Bert's cause.
    C. Drummond implied he would do it for free.
    D. The Philadelphia *Bulletin* has offered to support the endeavor.

ANSWER KEY - MULTIPLE CHOICE STUDY/QUIZ QUESTIONS
Inherit the Wind

Act One		Act Two		Act Three	
1.	B	15.	A	28.	B
2.	A	16.	C	29.	A
3.	C	17.	A	30.	D
4.	A	18.	B	31.	A
5.	A	19.	C	32.	A
6.	D	20.	B	33.	B
7.	B	21.	D	34.	D
8.	C	22.	B	35.	A
9.	D	23.	C	36.	A
10.	A	24.	A	37.	C
11.	C	25.	B		
12.	D	26.	C		
13.	B	27.	B		
14.	D				

PREREADING VOCABULARY WORKSHEETS

VOCABULARY - *Inherit the Wind*

Act One Part I: Using Prior Knowledge and Contextual Clues
   Below are the sentences in which the vocabulary words appear in the text. Read the sentence. Use any clues you can find in the sentence combined with your prior knowledge, and write what you think the underlined words mean on the lines provided.

1. Ahhh, your old man's a monkey! (Melinda gasps. She turns indignantly and runs off. . . .)

2. Rachael: (*Tentatively, calling*) Mr. Meeker . . . ?

3. I bet the Devil ain't so obliging.

4. The picnic table is in place. The sight of the food being uncovered is a magnetic attraction to Brady. He beams and moistens his lips) Ahhhh, what a handsome repast.

5. Has Mr. Cates ever tried to pollute your mind with his heathen dogma?

6. Henry Drummond, the agnostic?

7. He looks at the ring of faces, which have been disturbed by Brown's description of the heretic Drummond. . . .

8. A long ominous shadow appears across the buildings, cast from a figure approaching off stage.

9. Brady (With affable sarcasm): Is the counsel for the defense showing us the latest fashion in the great metropolitan city of Chicago?

10. I object to the note of levity which the counsel for the defense is introducing into these proceedings.

11. DRUMMOND: . . . Your Honor, I want that sign taken down! Or else I want another one put up--just as big, just as big letters--saying "Read Your Darwin!"
    JUDGE: That's preposterous!

12. It takes strength for a woman to love such a man. Especially when he's a pariah in the community.

Inherit the Wind Vocabulary Act One Part II

Part II: Determining the Meaning
You have tried to figure out the meanings of the vocabulary words for Act One, Scene One. Now match the vocabulary words to their dictionary definitions. If there are words for which you cannot figure out the definition by contextual clues and by process of elimination, look them up in a dictionary.

___ 1. indignantly
___ 2. tentatively
___ 3. obliging
___ 4. repast
___ 5. heathen
___ 6. agnostic
___ 7. heretic
___ 8. ominous
___ 9. affable
___ 10. levity
___ 11. preposterous
___ 12. pariah

A. Eager to do service for
B. Person who holds controversial opinions
C. With an anger aroused by something unjust
D. Threatening
E. One who believes there can be no proof of the existence of God but does not deny the possibility that God exists
F. Religion not acknowledging the God of Judaism, Christianity or Islam
G. Hesitantly; uncertainly
H. Feast
I. Absurd
J. Frivolity; lightness of manner and speech
K. Social outcast
L. Gentle; friendly

Vocabulary - *Inherit the Wind* Act Two

Part I: Using Prior Knowledge and Contextual Clues
   Below are the sentences in which the vocabulary words appear in the text. Read the sentence. Use any clues you can find in the sentence combined with your prior knowledge, and write what you think the underlined words mean on the lines provided.

13. I want people everywhere to know I bear no personal animosity toward Henry Drummond.

14. The crowd bursts out into an orgy of hosannahs and waving arms.

15. I know it is the great zeal of your faith which makes you utter this prayer! But it is possible to be overzealous to destroy that which you hope to save. . . .

16. May I remind you, Miss Brown, that you are testifying under oath, and it is unlawful to withhold pertinent information.

17. I am not in the least interested in the pagan hypotheses of that book.

18. Then how in perdition do you have the gall to whoop up this holy war against something you don't know anything about?

19. But your client is wrong! He is deluded! He has lost his way!

20. A couple of die-hard "Amens." Drummond ignores this glib gag.

21. Oh. You interpret that the first day recorded in the Book of Genesis could be of indeterminate length.

Inherit the Wind Vocabulary Act Two Part II

Part II: Determining the Meaning
You have tried to figure out the meanings of the vocabulary words for Act One Scene II - Act Two Scene I. Now match the vocabulary words to their dictionary definitions. If there are words for which you cannot figure out the definition by contextual clues and by process of elimination, look them up in a dictionary.

___ 13. animosity   A. Uncontrolled or immoderate indulgence in an activity
___ 14. orgy   B. Bitter hostility or hatred
___ 15. overzealous   C. Too full of enthusiasm for a cause
___ 16. pertinent   D. Deceived
___ 17. pagan   E. Performed with a natural, offhand ease
___ 18. perdition   F. That which relates to the matter at hand
___ 19. deluded   G. Eternal damnation
___ 20. glib   H. Not precisely established
___ 21. indeterminate   I. Not Christian, Moslem or Jewish

Vocabulary - *Inherit the Wind* Act Three

Part I: Using Prior Knowledge and Contextual Clues

Below are the sentences in which the vocabulary words appear in the text. Read the sentence. Use any clues you can find in the sentence combined with your prior knowledge, and write what you think the underlined words mean on the lines provided.

22. Brady re-enters and crosses ponderously to the Radio Man.

23. Court will reconvene in the case of the State versus Bertram Cates.

24. DRUMMOND: Is it not customary in this state to allow the defendant to make a statement before sentence is passed? . . .
    JUDGE: Colonel Drummond, I regret this omission.

25. From the hallowed hills of sacred Sinai, in the days of remote antiquity, came the law which has been our bulwark and our shield.

26. He freezes. His lips move, but nothing comes out. Paradoxically, his silence brings silence. The orator can hold his audience only by not speaking.

27. The sheaf of manuscript, clutched in his raised hand, scatters in mid air. The great words flutter innocuously to the courtroom floor.

28. Several men lift the prostrate Brady, and stretch him across three chairs.

29. Unloved children, of all ages, insinuate themselves/ Into spotlights and rotogravures.

30. And I know what you thought./ Let us leave the lamentations to the illiterate! Why should we weep for him? He cried enough for himself!

31. You hypocrite! You fraud!

Inherit the Wind Vocabulary Act Three Continued

32. Excuse me, gentlemen. I must get me to a typewriter
   And hammer out the story of an <u>atheist</u> who believes in God.

Part II: Determining the Meaning
    You have tried to figure out the meanings of the vocabulary words for Act Three. Now match the vocabulary words to their dictionary definitions. If there are words for which you cannot figure out the definition by contextual clues and by process of elimination, look them up in a dictionary.

___ 22. ponderously   A. As something exhibiting unexplainable or contradictory aspects

___ 23. reconvene   B. Statements of grief or mourning

___ 24. omission   C. One who says he believes one way but in actions shows or behaves the opposite

___ 25. bulwark   D. Lacking in grace; unwieldy from weight or bulk

___ 26. paradoxically   E. Something serving as a defense

___ 27. innocuously   F. Imply

___ 28. prostrate   G. One who does not believe in God

___ 29. insinuate   H. Harmlessly

___ 30. lamentations   I. Come together again for a formal purpose

___ 31. hypocrite   J. Something that is left out

___ 32. atheist   K. Lying flat

ANSWER KEY: VOCABULARY - *Inherit the Wind*

<u>Act One</u>
1. C
2. G
3. A
4. H
5. F
6. E
7. B
8. D
9. L
10. J
11. I
12. K

<u>Act Two</u>
13. B
14. A
15. C
16. F
17. I
18. G
19. D
20. E
21. H

<u>Act Three</u>
22. D
23. I
24. J
25. E
26. A
27. H
28. K
29. F
30. B
31. C
32. G

DAILY LESSONS

LESSON ONE

Objectives
1. To introduce the *Inherit the Wind* unit
2. To distribute books and other related materials

Activity #1
Distribute Writing Assignment #1. Discuss the directions in detail and give students ample time to complete the assignment.

Activity #2
While students are working, distribute the materials students will use in this unit. After students finish writing, explain in detail how they are to use these materials.

Study Guides Students should read the study guide questions for each reading assignment prior to beginning the reading assignment to get a feeling for what events and ideas are important in the section they are about to read. After reading the section, students will (as a class or individually) answer the questions to review the important events and ideas from that section of the book. Students should keep the study guides as study materials for the unit test.

Vocabulary Prior to reading a reading assignment, students will do vocabulary work related to the section of the book they are about to read. Following the completion of the reading of the book, there will be a vocabulary review of all the words used in the vocabulary assignments. Students should keep their vocabulary work as study materials for the unit test.

Reading Assignment Sheet You need to fill in the reading assignment sheet to let students know by when their reading has to be completed. You can either write the assignment sheet up on a side blackboard or bulletin board and leave it there for students to see each day, or you can "ditto" copies for each student to have. In either case, you should advise students to become very familiar with the reading assignments so they know what is expected of them.

Extra Activities Center The Extra Activities page of this unit contains suggestions for an extra library of related books and articles in your classroom as well as crossword and word search puzzles. Make an extra activities center in your room where you will keep these materials for students to use. (Bring the books and articles in from the library and keep several copies of the puzzles on hand.) Explain to students that these materials are available for students to use when they finish reading assignments or other class work early.

Nonfiction Assignment Sheet Explain to students that they each are to read at least one non-fiction piece from the in-class library at some time during the unit. Students will fill out a nonfiction assignment sheet after completing the reading to help you evaluate their reading experiences and to help the students think about and evaluate their own reading experiences.

NONFICTION ASSIGNMENT SHEET
(To be completed after reading the required nonfiction article)

Name _____ Date _____

Title of Nonfiction Read _____

Written By _____ Publication Date _____

I. Factual Summary: Write a short summary of the piece you read.

II. Vocabulary
    1. With which vocabulary words in the piece did you encounter some degree of difficulty?

    2. How did you resolve your lack of understanding with these words?

III. Interpretation: What was the main point the author wanted you to get from reading his work?

IV. Criticism
    1. With which points of the piece did you agree or find easy to accept? Why?

    2. With which points of the piece did you disagree or find difficult to believe? Why?

V. Personal Response: What do you think about this piece? OR How does this piece influence your ideas?

WRITING ASSIGNMENT #1 - *Inherit the Wind*

PROMPT

As you probably know by now, there are many theories about how people came to exist. The two main theories are called creationism and evolution. Creationism is the theory that God created man in his own image, as is set forth in The Bible. Evolution is the theory that man evolved over millions of years from tiny life cells to monkeys and finally to man as we are today. Some people believe that both of these theories are possible at the same time; in other words, they believe no one knows exactly how long it took God to make man nor how He did it--perhaps He did it through evolution.

Your assignment is to write a composition in which you state your own views on the subject. How do *you* think man came to exist? Do you believe in creationism, evolution, a combination of the two, or something else entirely?

PREWRITING

The best way to begin is to stop and think about what you *do* believe. Once you decide that, then write down a couple of good reasons *why* you believe that.

DRAFTING

Write a paragraph in which you introduce your ideas about how people came to exist.

In the body of your composition, write one paragraph for each of the reasons why you believe what you believe. Use a topic sentence for each paragraph and fill out the paragraph with examples and explanations to support your reasoning.

Write a paragraph in which you draw your conclusions and bring your composition to a close.

PROMPT

When you finish the rough draft of your paper, ask a student who sits near you to read it. After reading your rough draft, he/she should tell you what he/she liked best about your work, which parts were difficult to understand, and ways in which your work could be improved. Reread your paper considering your critic's comments and make the corrections you think are necessary.

PROOFREADING

Do a final proofreading of your paper double-checking your grammar, spelling, organization, and the clarity of your ideas.

LESSON TWO

Objectives
1. To preview the study questions for Act One
2. To familiarize students with the vocabulary for Act One
3. To make the reading part assignments
4. To give students time to practice their reading parts

Activity #1

Show students how to preview the study questions and do the vocabulary worksheets. Give students about 15 minutes to complete the vocabulary worksheets for Act One.

Activity #2

Distribute the Reading Parts Assignment Sheet. Tell students which parts they have been assigned to read. Explain that they will be reading the play orally and that they will be given a grade for their reading part in the play. Tell students that they have the remainder of this class period to practice their reading parts with the others in their reading section.

LESSON THREE

Objectives
1. To read Act One, Scene One
2. To evaluate students' reading skills

Activity

Have students read Act One, Scene One, of *Inherit the Wind* orally in class with each student reading the part he/she has been assigned. If you have not yet completed an oral reading evaluation for your students this marking period, this would be a good opportunity to do so. A form is included with this unit for your convenience.

ORAL READING EVALUATION - *Inherit the Wind*

Name _____ Class____ Date _____

SKILL	EXCELLENT	GOOD	AVERAGE	FAIR	POOR
Fluency	5	4	3	2	1
Clarity	5	4	3	2	1
Audibility	5	4	3	2	1
Pronunciation	5	4	3	2	1
_____	5	4	3	2	1
_____	5	4	3	2	1

Total _____   Grade _____

Comments:

LESSON FOUR

Objectives
1. To read Act One Scene Two
2. To review the main ideas and events of Act One
3. To preview the study questions and vocabulary for Act Two

Activity #1

Have students read Act One Scene Two orally in class with each student reading the part he/she has been assigned. Continue the oral reading evaluations.

Activity #2

Give students a few minutes to formulate answers for the study guide questions for Act One and then discuss the answers to the questions in detail. Write the answers on the board or overhead transparency so students can have the correct answers for study purposes. NOTE: It is a good practice in public speaking and leadership skills for individual students to take charge of leading the discussions of the study questions. Perhaps a different student could go to the front of the class and lead the discussion each day that the study questions are discussed during this unit. Of course, the teacher should guide the discussion when appropriate and be sure to fill in any gaps the students leave.

Activity #3

Give students about fifteen minutes to preview the study questions for Act Two of *Inherit the Wind* and to do the related vocabulary work.

LESSON FIVE

Objectives
1. To read Act Two
2. To evaluate students' reading skills

Activity

Have students read Act Two of *Inherit the Wind* orally in class with each student reading the part he/she has been assigned. Continue the oral reading evaluations.

LESSON SIX

Objectives
    1. To finish reading Act Two
    2. To review the main ideas and events from Act Two
    3. To preview the study questions and vocabulary for Act Three

Activity #1
    Have students finish reading Act Two orally in class with each student reading the part he/she has been assigned. Continue the oral reading evaluations.

Activity #2
    Give students a few minutes to formulate answers to the study guide questions for Act Two, and then discuss the answers to the questions together with the class. Students should take notes for study use later.

Activity #3
    Tell students that prior to the next class meeting they should preview the study questions and do the prereading vocabulary work for Act Three.

LESSON SEVEN

Objectives
    1. To read Act Three
    2. To evaluate students' reading skills

Activity
    Have students read Act Three orally in class with each student reading the part he/she has been assigned. Continue the oral reading evaluations.

LESSON EIGHT

Objectives
1. To review the main ideas and events from Act Three
2. To discuss *Inherit the Wind* on interpretive and critical levels

Activity #1
Give students a few minutes to formulate answers to the study questions for Act Three. Discuss the answers to the questions with your class. Students should take notes for study use.

Activity #2
Choose the questions from the Extra Discussion Questions/Writing Assignments which seem most appropriate for your students. A class discussion of these questions is most effective if students have been given the opportunity to formulate answers to the questions prior to the discussion. To this end, you may either have all the students formulate answers to all the questions, divide your class into groups and assign one or more questions to each group, or assign one question to each student in your class. The option you choose will make a difference in the amount of class time needed for this activity.

After students have had ample time to formulate answers to the questions, begin your class discussion of the questions and the ideas presented by the questions. Be sure students take notes during the discussion so they have information to study for the unit test.

EXTRA WRITING ASSIGNMENTS/DISCUSSION QUESTIONS - *Inherit the Wind*

Interpretation

1. What are the conflicts in the play, and how are they resolved?

2. What issues are on trial in *Inherit the Wind*?

3. Where is the climax of the play? Explain your choice.

4. Are the characters in *Inherit the Wind* stereotypes? If so, explain the usefulness of employing stereotypes in the play. If they are not, explain how they merit individuality.

5. What is the setting of the play? What time and place were chosen as the setting? Why?

6. What was Rachael's testimony? What effect did it have on the outcome of the trial?

Critical

7. Compare and contrast Drummond and Brady.

8. Characterize the authors' style of writing. How does it contribute to the value of the novel?

9. How did Rachael change during the play?

10. Give a character analysis of Mr. Hornbeck.

11. Explain Mr. Hornbeck's role in the play.

12. Explain how the title, *Inherit the Wind*, is appropriate.

13. Explain how the opening lines between Howard and Melinda set the stage for the rest of the play.

14. Who was responsible for Brady's death? Explain your choice.

15. What is Howard's role in the play? (How is he important to the ideas and themes of the play?)

16. Give a character analysis of Brady.

Inherit the Wind Extra Discussion Questions page 2

17. Explain why the Radio Man is included in the play.

18. Compare and contrast Drummond and Hornbeck.

19. What are the various views of religion presented in the play?

20. What are the various views of education presented in the play?

21. Explain how and why the crowd's opinions changed.

22. There is an old saying that "behind every great man there is a great woman." Is this true in the case of the Bradys? Explain your answer.

23. Is the case presented in the play realistic? Is it believable? If so, how? If not, why not?

24. Judges are supposed to be impartial, but they are human, too. Examine the judge's role in the trial.

Personal Response

25. Did you enjoy reading *Inherit the Wind*? Why or why not?

26. Who should decide what will be taught in schools? Why?

27. Was justice served in *Inherit the Wind*? That is, did Cates get what he deserved?

28. What do you think will happen with the appeal? Why?

LESSON NINE

Objective
To review all of the vocabulary work done in this unit

Activity
Choose one (or more) of the vocabulary review activities listed below and spend your class period as directed in the activity. Some of the materials for these review activities are located in the Vocabulary Resources section of this unit.

VOCABULARY REVIEW ACTIVITIES

1. Divide your class into two teams and have an old-fashioned spelling or definition bee.

2. Give each of your students (or students in groups of two, three, or four) an *Inherit the Wind* Vocabulary Word Search Puzzle. The person (group) to find all of the vocabulary words in the puzzle first wins.

3. Give students an *Inherit the Wind* Vocabulary Word Search Puzzle without the word list. The person or group to find the most vocabulary words in the puzzle wins.

4. Use an *Inherit the Wind* Vocabulary Crossword Puzzle. Put the puzzle onto a transparency on the overhead projector (so everyone can see it), and do the puzzle together as a class.

5. Give students an *Inherit the Wind* Vocabulary Matching Worksheet to do.

6. Divide your class into two teams. Use the *Inherit the Wind* vocabulary words with their letters jumbled as a word list. Student 1 from Team A faces off against Student 1 from Team B. You write the first jumbled word on the board. The first student (1A or 1B) to unscramble the word wins the chance for his/her team to score points. If 1A wins the jumble, go to student 2A and give him/her a definition. He/she must give you the correct spelling of the vocabulary word which fits that definition. If he/she does, Team A scores a point, and you give student 3A a definition for which you expect a correctly spelled matching vocabulary word. Continue giving Team A definitions until some team member makes an incorrect response. An incorrect response sends the game back to the jumbled-word face off, this time with students 2A and 2B. Instead of repeating giving definitions to the first few students of each team, continue with the student after the one who gave the last incorrect response on the team. For example, if Team B wins the jumbled-word face-off, and student 5B gave the last incorrect answer for Team B, you would start this round of definition questions with student 6B, and so on. The team with the most points wins!

7. Have students write a story in which they correctly use as many vocabulary words as possible. Have students read their compositions orally! Post the most original compositions on your bulletin board.

LESSON TEN

Objective
  To widen the breadth of students' knowledge of the topics discussed or touched upon in *Inherit the Wind*

Activity
  Take students to the library. Tell students that they are to choose a topic related to *Inherit the Wind* and find and read at least two different articles relating to that topic. They may use one of the suggested topics or think of a topic of their own choice. If your library has a well-stocked media center, perhaps students could have the option of finding related information on video tape or other media. Students should take notes and fill out a Nonfiction Assignment Sheet for each article they read. Offer extra credit, bonus points, or other incentives for students who read more than two articles.

Suggested Topics
Darwin's *Origin of the Species*
Biographical Information about Darwin
Separation of Church and State
Recent Conflicts About What Will be Taught/Read in Schools
The Foundation of Public Education
Critical Reviews of *Inherit the Wind*
Evolutionism
Creationism

LESSON ELEVEN

Objectives
  1. To give students the opportunity to finish reading their articles
  2. To give students the chance to exchange ideas in a small group setting
  3. To get students to express their ideas orally to others and to listen to other students' ideas (speaking and listening skills)

Activity #1
  If your students need more time to read their articles (couldn't take them from the library or copy them), use the first part of this class period to finish reading.

Activity #2
  Using the suggested topic list above, find out which students chose each of the topics listed and have them get together in small groups. (All students who read about Darwin should get together. All students who read critical reviews of *Inherit the Wind* should get together, etc.)
  In these small groups, students should tell each other what articles they read and the basic content of each article. After doing so, they should compare and discuss their articles.

LESSONS TWELVE

Objectives
1. To help prepare students for an oral discussion of the topics in the nonfiction reading assignment
2. To give students the opportunity to practice writing to inform
3. To give the teacher the opportunity to evaluate students' writing skills

Activity
Distribute Writing Assignment #2. Discuss the directions in detail and give students ample time to complete the assignment.

LESSON THIRTEEN

Objectives
1. To discuss the topics from the nonfiction reading assignment
2. To expose all students to a wealth of information relating to the ideas in *Inherit the Wind*
3. To give students the opportunity to practice public speaking

Activity
Ask each student to give a brief oral report about the nonfiction work he/she read for the nonfiction reading assignment. Your criteria for evaluating this report will vary depending on the level of your students. You may wish for students to give a complete report without using notes of any kind, or you may want students to read directly from a written report, or you may want to do something in between these two extremes. Just make students aware of your criteria in ample time for them to prepare their reports.

Start with one student's report. After that, ask if anyone else in the class has read on a topic related to the first student's report. If no one has, choose another student at random. After each report, be sure to ask if anyone has a report related to the one just completed. That will help keep a continuity during the discussion of the reports. Use the reports as springboards for discussions of the topics covered.

WRITING ASSIGNMENT #2 - *Inherit the Wind*

PROMPT
You have collected a substantial amount of information about a topic related to *Inherit the Wind*. In the next class period you will be asked to give an oral presentation about that information. To help you prepare your presentation and collect and organize your thoughts, your assignment is to write a composition in which you summarize the information you have found relating to your topic.

PREWRITING
Most of your prewriting work has been done as you took notes about the information you read. What you need to do now is to review your notes and categorize the information you have found. Go through your notes and make a list of all the kinds of information you have. Then, turn your list into an outline form, grouping like things together and organizing the information so that one idea can flow into another.

DRAFTING
Write an introductory paragraph in which you introduce your topic.
In the body of your composition, write one paragraph for each of the main points you found in your reading. Fill out each paragraph with explanations and/or examples to support your statements.
Write a final paragraph in which you make your conclusions and bring your composition to a close.

PROMPT
When you finish the rough draft of your paper, ask a student who sits near you to read it. After reading your rough draft, he/she should tell you what he/she liked best about your work, which parts were difficult to understand, and ways in which your work could be improved. Reread your paper considering your critic's comments and make the corrections you think are necessary.

PROOFREADING
Do a final proofreading of your paper double-checking your grammar, spelling, organization, and the clarity of your ideas.

LESSONS FOURTEEN AND FIFTEEN

Objective
   To bring in the facts about the Scopes Trial and the people who were involved in it

NOTE: If your students have covered this material thoroughly in the nonfiction reading reports, you may want to skip these two lessons.

A special thanks to Compton's Learning Company for giving us permission to reprint these articles from the *Compton's Interactive Encyclopedia*.

Activity
   Have students read the nonfiction articles which follow. After the reading, hold a discussion of the facts and students' reactions to the articles.

LESSON SIXTEEN

Objectives
   1. To give students practice writing to persuade
   2. To give the teacher the opportunity to evaluate students' writing skills

Activity
   Distribute Writing Assignment #3. Discuss the directions in detail and give students ample time to complete the assignment.

   While students are working on Writing Assignment #3, call individual students to your desk or some other private area for individual writing conferences based on the first two writing assignments in this unit. An evaluation form is included with this unit to help you structure your conferences.

LESSON SEVENTEEN

Objective
   To review the main ideas presented in *Inherit the Wind*

Activity #1
   Choose one of the review games/activities included in the section and spend your class period as outlined there. Some materials for these activities are located in the Unit Resource section of this unit.

Activity #2
   Remind students that the Unit Test will be in the next class meeting. Stress the review of the Study Guides and their class notes as a last-minute, brush-up review for homework.

FACTUAL INFORMATION ABOUT DARWIN, THE SCOPES TRIAL, THE TWO ATTORNEYS WHO TRIED THE CASE AND THE REPORTER

SCOPES TRIAL, Dayton, Tenn., in 1925, famous case in which theory of evolution was upheld by Clarence Darrow, for defense, against William Jennings Bryan, prosecutor; John Scopes, biology teacher, was fined $100 in test of state law against teaching evolution in public schools; verdict reversed on technicality

DARROW, Clarence (1857-1938). Probably the most celebrated American lawyer of the 20th century, Clarence Darrow worked as defense counsel in many widely publicized trials, earning a permanent place in the annals of legal history. His fame did not decline over the years: in the 1970s his life was the subject of a one-man stage production starring Henry Fonda.

Darrow was born on April 18, 1857, near Kinsman, Ohio. He attended Allegheny College and the University of Michigan briefly before being admitted to the Ohio bar in 1878. In 1887 he moved to Chicago, where he soon was appointed city corporation counsel and later the general attorney for the Chicago and Northwestern Railroad. He resigned this position in 1895 to defend Eugene V. Debs, president of the American Railway Union, and other union leaders who had been arrested on a federal charge of contempt of court over difficulties arising out of the Pullman strike of 1894. Through this trial Darrow established a national reputation as a labor and criminal lawyer.

In 1902 President Theodore Roosevelt appointed him an arbitrator in the Pennsylvania anthracite coal strike. In 1907 he secured the acquittal of labor organizer William D. "Big Bill" Haywood for the murder of former Idaho governor Frank Steunenberg. After World War I he defended war protesters charged with violating state sedition laws.

The two most famous trials in which he participated took place in the 1920s. The first was the notorious Leopold-Loeb murder case of 1924. He saved Nathan Leopold and Richard Loeb from execution-but not from prison-for the murder of 14-year-old Robert Franks. In 1925 Darrow defended high school teacher John T. Scopes, who was charged with violating Tennessee law by teaching evolution. The prosecuting attorney in this famous "monkey trial" was William Jennings Bryan.

In his writings and speeches Darrow promoted freedom of expression and the closed shop for unions. He opposed capital punishment and Prohibition. He died in Chicago on March 13, 1938.

BRYAN, William Jennings (1860-1925). Although he was defeated three times for the presidency of the United States, William Jennings Bryan molded public opinion as few presidents have done. For many years he was the leader of the Democratic party, and it was his influence that won the Democratic presidential nomination for Woodrow Wilson in 1912.

Bryan was born in Salem, Ill. He went to school and practiced law in Illinois until 1887, when he moved to Nebraska. There he built up a reputation as a great orator and was elected to Congress.

Six years later, in 1896 at the age of 36, Bryan achieved national fame-he received his first nomination for the presidency. He won in the national Democratic convention by a vigorous appeal for free and unlimited coinage of silver. Turning to those who wanted only gold as the money standard, he exclaimed: "You shall not press down upon the brow of labor this crown of thorns. You shall not crucify mankind upon this cross of gold."

Though Bryan lost the election then and again in 1900 and 1908, he was still regarded as the leader of the Democratic party. Through his paper, called The Commoner, and by lectures delivered from Chautauqua platforms he advanced the cause of prohibition, of religion, and of morality.

Bryan was named secretary of state by President Wilson. He negotiated treaties with 30 countries, representing three fourths of the world's population, for investigation of disputes before resorting to war. Because of his opposition to war, he resigned from office in June 1915 in protest against the president's firmness concerning the sinking of the Lusitania.

After the war he moved to Florida and worked to advance moral and religious causes. He died in July 1925, in Dayton, Tenn., where he had been helping prosecute a case involving an "anti-evolution" law.

DARWIN AND EVOLUTION   Evolution was not a new idea, even in Darwin's day. Long before the time of Christ, philosophers had explained the great variety of plants and animals by proposing "natural" ways they could have developed. Before 1600 Sir Walter Raleigh concluded that dogs had turned into wolves and that the different races of men were related. Several philosophers also declared that new conditions caused plants to change into new varieties or species.

Georges-Louis Leclerc, comte de Buffon (1707-1788), went still further. In his 36-volume 'Natural History', he declared that modern animals had evolved, or "degenerated," from others and so on back to the beginning. Some changes, he thought, were produced when different forms interbred; others were caused by food, climate, pressure, and so on. According to Buffon's theory, the hippopotamus and elephant are large because their ancestors ate a great deal of food; the hair of lions is tawny because it has been bleached by the brilliant sunlight of the tropical plains.

Jean-Baptiste Lamarck (1744-1829) maintained that plants and animals evolved because of an inborn tendency to progress from simple to complex forms. Environment, however, modified this progression and so did use or disuse of parts. Giraffes, for example, developed long necks by straining to reach the leaves of trees; snakes lost their legs by crawling. Birds, said Lamarck, came from hairy ancestors. Their attempts to fly forced air into the hairs and so turned them into feathers.

Darwin knew about these attempts to explain evolution. His grandfather, Erasmus Darwin, had published several books containing ideas much like Lamarck's theory of use and disuse. He felt, however, that early writers on the subject had speculated too much and had collected too few facts. As a result, they failed to convince the scientific world that evolution had actually taken place. They also failed to give a reasonable explanation of how changes might have produced the different organisms found upon the earth today.

Darwin determined to avoid these mistakes and to collect and test facts scientifically before explaining them. After his return to England he followed this course for 15 months, meanwhile also writing up the 'Journal' of his scientific work on the Beagle.

Then he happened to read 'An Essay on the Principle of Population', by a British economist, Thomas Malthus. Malthus undertook to prove that human populations tend to increase more rapidly than food and other necessities. The result is a struggle in which some people succeed and become wealthy while others fail or even starve.

Darwin applied this theory to the world of nature. Plants and animals, he knew, reproduce so rapidly that the earth could not hold them if all their young survived. This meant that there was a constant struggle for space, food, and shelter, as well as against enemies and unfavorable conditions. Young trees, for example, struggle for space. Those that grow most rapidly survive while those that grow slowly become stunted and die. Certain hawks struggle, or compete, with each other for the mice they eat, and the poorest hunters go hungry. Mice, in turn, struggle to keep from being caught by hawks. In frigid winters all living things struggle against cold. Some endure it and others keep themselves warm, but many die because they can do neither.

Struggling and living or dying could not lead to evolution if all members of each living kind or species were exactly alike. Darwin found that members of a single species vary greatly in shape, size, color, strength, and so on. He also believed that most of these variations could be inherited.

Under the constant struggle to exist, organisms with harmful variations were almost sure to die before they could have young ones. Living things with useful variations, however, survived and reproduced. When their descendants varied still more, the process was repeated. In other words, the struggle for existence selected organisms with helpful variations but made others die out. This was the critical point in Darwin's reasoning.

This natural selection had two further effects that were important. Many newly developed organisms remained in their old habitats, where they struggled successfully against older forms, crowding them out of existence. Other new organisms made their way into different surroundings, where they prospered and kept on changing. Over the ages, these two factors produced a steady succession of new plants, animals, and other organisms. They enabled living things to go into all sorts of environments and become fitted, or adapted, to many different types of life. Thus mammals, which started out on dry land, also spread into swamps, lakes, and seas. Some climbed trees, some burrowed, and some even learned to fly.

Darwin wrote a short sketch of his theory in 1842 and a longer one in 1844. Instead of publishing the second statement, however, he continued to collect information. He also took time to write books on coral reefs, volcanic islands, barnacles, and the geology of South America. Not until 1856 did he begin what would have been a three- or four-volume book on the subject of evolution.

In 1858 he received a manuscript from a young naturalist, Alfred Russel Wallace, who also had developed a theory of natural selection. Although Darwin was willing to withdraw in favor of Wallace, associates insisted that he publish his own discoveries without further delay. With Wallace's approval, short statements by both men were published late in 1858. Darwin went on to write his famous book 'On the Origin of Species by Means of Natural Selection', which appeared in 1859.

After completing the 'Origin of Species', Darwin began 'The Variation of Animals and Plants under Domestication', which showed how rapidly some organisms had evolved under artificial, instead of natural, selection. 'The Descent of Man', published in 1871, elaborated the theory of sexual selection and applied Lamarck's unsound theory of use and disuse (see Lamarck). Later books dealt with earthworms, orchids, climbing plants, and plants that eat insects. 'The Power of Movement in Plants' was written with the help of Darwin's son Francis, who became a botanist. Another son, George, was an astronomer and Horace was a noted engineer.

Darwin, who was a semi-invalid for much of his life, became very weak in 1881 and complained that he no longer could work. He died on April 19, 1882, and was buried among England's greatest men in Westminster Abbey.

Darwin himself never claimed to provide proof of evolution or of the origin of species. His claim was that if evolution had occurred, a number of otherwise mysterious facts about plants and animals could be easily explained. Recently, however, direct evidence of evolution has been observed, and evolution is now supported by a wealth of evidence from a variety of scientific fields.

In spite of this evidence, evolution has been rejected by the members of certain religious groups who prefer what they term the theory of creationism. This attempts to explain some features of plant and animal life through a literal interpretation of the Bible. In the scientific community, however, there is little doubt that the general outline of Darwin's theory of evolution is correct.

A recently proposed modification of evolutionary theory suggests that from time to time evolution may proceed relatively rapidly. These bursts of activity are then followed by long periods of little change. This modification, called punctuated equilibrium, goes a long way toward explaining what has been called the incompleteness of the fossil record; that is, the scarcity of fossils intermediate between earlier and later members of the same plant or animal family.

MENCKEN, H.L. (1880-1956). The Sage of Baltimore, as H.L. Mencken was called, was a newspaper columnist and essayist whose outrageous wit and biting sarcasm made him the center of controversy most of his life. He derided nearly everything American-government, religion, education, the judiciary, business, and more-yet he considered himself a devoted patriot who happened to have the good sense to remain in a country where nearly everything that happened was a cause for mirth and derision. It was he who coined the term boobus Americanus to describe the average citizen. Yet, for all his complaining, he exerted a great influence on the literature of his day, and he also became the leading authority on American English. His 'The American Language', published in 1919, is still a classic on the subject.

Henry Louis Mencken was born in Baltimore on Sept. 12, 1880. He graduated from the Baltimore Polytechnic Institute (a high school) in 1899 and went to work on the Baltimore Morning Herald as a police reporter. In 1906 he joined the staff of the Baltimore Sun, with which he remained associated most of his life. From 1914 until 1923 he was co-editor, with George Jean Nathan, of the Smart Set, an influential literary magazine. He had been book reviewer for the magazine since 1908. In 1924 he helped found the American Mercury and remained as editor until 1933.

Many of Mencken's essays were collected in a series of six volumes titled collectively 'Prejudices' (1919-27). Changes in the United States and the rest of the world wrought by the Depression lessened the appeal of Mencken's witty criticisms, and he never regained the influence he had wielded earlier. He nevertheless continued to publish. He suffered a stroke in 1948 and never fully recovered. He died on Jan. 29, 1956. Some of his best essays were later collected in 'American Scene' (1965), edited by Huntington Cairns.

--- Courtesy of Compton's Learning Company

MENCKEN ON DARWIN
from The Baltimore *Evening Sun*, April 6, 1931

THE TROUBLE with human progress is that it tends to go too fast--that is, too fast for the great majority of comfortable and incurious men. Its agents are always in a hurry, and so become unpopular. If Darwin had printed "The Origin of the Species" as a serial running twenty or thirty years he might have found himself, at the end of it, a member of the House of Lords or even Archbishop of Canterbury. But he disgorged it in one stupendous and appalling dose, and in consequence he alarmed millions, including many of his fellow scientists, and got an evil name. To this day, though all of the soundest (and thus most revolutionary) of his ideas have become platitudes, he continues to be thought of much as Simon Legree, Thomas Paine and John Wilkes Booth are thought of. To name a new public-school after him would cause almost as grave a scandal as to name it after Lillian Russell. In at least two-thirds of the American States one of the easiest ways to get into public office is to denounce him as a scoundrel. But by the year 2030, I daresay, what remains of his doctrine, if anything, will be accepted as complacently as the Copernican cosmography is now accepted. His offense was simply that he was too precipitate.

WRITING ASSIGNMENT #3 - *Inherit the Wind*

PROMPT
You have read H. L. Mencken's article about Darwin from the Baltimore *Evening Sun*. In it he says that by the year 2030 Darwin's doctrine (or what remains of it) will be commonly accepted. Here we are more than halfway from 1931 to 2030. Your assignment is to write a composition in which you persuade me that Mencken was right or Mencken was wrong.

PREWRITING
First, decide what you think. Do you think Mencken was right and that by 2030 Darwin's doctrine will be commonly accepted, or do you think there will still be a raging debate over evolution versus creation? Why do you think that? Write down at least three good reasons. Next to each reason, jot down some examples or facts to support your statements.

DRAFTING
Write an introductory paragraph in which you introduce the idea that Mencken was right (or wrong).

In the body of your composition, write one paragraph for each of your reasons. Use a topic sentence for each paragraph and fill out each paragraph with examples and facts to support your statements.

Write a concluding paragraph in which you summarize your ideas and bring your composition to a close.

PROMPT
When you finish the rough draft of your paper, ask a student who sits near you to read it. After reading your rough draft, he/she should tell you what he/she liked best about your work, which parts were difficult to understand, and ways in which your work could be improved. Reread your paper considering your critic's comments and make the corrections you think are necessary.

PROOFREADING
Do a final proofreading of your paper double-checking your grammar, spelling, organization, and the clarity of your ideas.

WRITING EVALUATION FORM - *Inherit the Wind*

Name _____ Date _____

      Grade _____

Circle One For Each Item:

Grammar: correct   errors noted on paper

Spelling: correct   errors noted on paper

Punctuation: correct   errors noted on paper

Legibility: excellent   good   fair   poor

Strengths:

Weaknesses:

Comments/Suggestions:

REVIEW GAMES/ACTIVITIES - *Inherit the Wind*

1. Ask the class to make up a unit test for *Inherit the Wind*. The test should have 4 sections: matching, true/false, short answer, and essay. Students may use 1/2 period to make the test and then swap papers and use the other 1/2 class period to take a test a classmate has devised (open book). You may want to use the unit test included in this section or take questions from the students' unit tests to formulate your own test.

2. Take 1/2 period for students to make up true and false questions (including the answers). Collect the papers and divide the class into two teams. Draw a big tic-tac-toe board on the chalk board. Make one team X and one team O. Ask questions to each side, giving each student one turn. If the question is answered correctly, that students' team's letter (X or O) is placed in the box. If the answer is incorrect, no mark is placed in the box. The object is to get three marks in a row like tic-tac-toe. You may want to keep track of the number of games won for each team.

3. Take 1/2 period for students to make up questions (true/false and short answer). Collect the questions. Divide the class into two teams. You'll alternate asking questions to individual members of teams A & B (like in a spelling bee). The question keeps going from A to B until it is correctly answered, then a new question is asked. A correct answer does not allow the team to get another question. Correct answers are +2 points; incorrect answers are -1 point.

4. Have students pair up and quiz each other from their study guides and class notes.

5. Give students an *Inherit the Wind* crossword puzzle to complete.

6. Divide your class into two teams. Use the *Inherit the Wind* crossword words with their letters jumbled as a word list. Student 1 from Team A faces off against Student 1 from Team B. You write the first jumbled word on the board. The first student (1A or 1B) to unscramble the word wins the chance for his/her team to score points. If 1A wins the jumble, go to student 2A and give him/her a clue. He/she must give you the correct word which matches that clue. If he/she does, Team A scores a point, and you give student 3A a clue for which you expect another correct response. Continue giving Team A clues until some team member makes an incorrect response. An incorrect response sends the game back to the jumbled-word face off, this time with students 2A and 2B. Instead of repeating giving clues to the first few students of each team, continue with the student after the one who gave the last incorrect response on the team. For example, if Team B wins the jumbled-word face-off, and student 5B gave the last incorrect answer for Team B, you would start this round of clue questions with student 6B, and so on. The team with the most points wins!

UNIT TESTS

SHORT ANSWER UNIT TEST 1 - *Inherit the Wind*

I. Matching/Identify

___ 1. Melinda   A. Chief prosecutor in this case

___ 2. Howard   B. Brown's daughter

___ 3. Drummond   C. Reverend

___ 4. Brady   D. Circuit District Attorney

___ 5. Rachael   E. Howard called her & her family "worms"

___ 6. Cates   F. Bailiff

___ 7. Hornbeck   G. Reporter from the Baltimore *Herald*

___ 8. Brown   H. Attorney for the defense

___ 9. Meeker   I. Boy exposed to Darwin's ideas

___ 10. Davenport   J. Was jailed for teaching about Darwin

II. Short answer

1. What did Darwin's *Origin* say?

2. What kind of a man does E. K. Hornbeck appear to be?

3. What does Drummond accomplish on the first day of the trial?

4. What explanation does Drummond give Bert as to why people look at him "worse than a murderer"?

Inherit the Wind Short Answer Unit Test 1 Page 2

5. What does Rev. Brown pray for when Rachael asks him not to damn Bert?

6. What does Drummond try to establish when questioning Howard?

7. Why did Bert leave the church?

8. What problem did Drummond have with his expert witnesses?

9. As a last resort, who does Drummond call to the witness stand? Why?

10. Why did Drummond want Brady to admit that the first day could have been 25 hours long?

11. Identify Golden Dancer.

Inherit the Wind Short Answer Unit Test 1 Page 3

12. Did Bert win or lose?

13. To what does Rachael compare ideas?

14. Drummond says Brady had the same right as Cates. What right is that?

Inherit the Wind Short Answer Unit Test 1 Page 4

III. Composition

What is the point of *Inherit the Wind*? When we read books, we usually come away from our reading experience a little richer, having given more thought to a particular aspect of life. What do you think Lawrence and Lee intended us to gain from reading this play?

IV. Vocabulary

Listen to the vocabulary words and write them down. Go back later and fill in the correct definition for each word.

1.

2.

3.

4.

5.

6.

7.

8.

9.

10.

SHORT ANSWER UNIT TEST 2 - *Inherit the Wind*

I. Matching/Identify

___ 1. Melinda   A. Bailiff

___ 2. Howard   B. Attorney for the defense

___ 3. Drummond   C. Circuit District Attorney

___ 4. Brady   D. Reverend

___ 5. Rachael   E. Was jailed for teaching about Darwin

___ 6. Cates   F. Chief prosecutor in this case

___ 7. Hornbeck   G. Boy exposed to Darwin's ideas

___ 8. Brown   H. Brown's daughter

___ 9. Meeker   I. Reporter from the Baltimore *Herald*

___ 10. Davenport   J. Howard called her & her family "worms"

II. Short Answer

1. Why was Bert Cates in jail?

2. What is Brady's reaction to Brown's damnation of his own daughter?

3. What does Drummond try to establish when questioning Howard?

Inherit the Wind Short Answer Unit Test 2 Page 2

4. What problem did Drummond have with his expert witnesses?

5. As a last resort, who does Drummond call to the witness stand? Why?

6. What does Drummond gain by questioning the belief in the literal translation of the Bible?

7. Why did Drummond want Brady to admit that the first day could have been 25 hours long?

8. What was the jury's verdict?

9. Did Bert win or lose?

10. To what does Rachael compare ideas?

11. Drummond says Brady had the same right as Cates. What right is that?

Inherit the Wind Short Answer Unit Test 2 Page 3

III. Composition
Write complete answers to each of the following questions:

1. Compare and contrast Drummond and Brady.

2. What was Rachael's testimony, and what effect did it have on the outcome of the trial?

3. What was Mr. Hornbeck's role in the play? Why was his character important?

4. What issue(s) were on trial in *Inherit the Wind*, and what effect did the outcome of the trial have on each?

Inherit the Wind Short Answer Unit Test 2 Page 4

IV. Vocabulary

Listen to the vocabulary words and write them down. Go back later and fill in the correct definition for each word.

1.

2.

3.

4.

5.

6.

7.

8.

9.

10.

KEY: SHORT ANSWER UNIT TESTS - *Inherit the Wind*

The short answer questions are taken directly from the study guides.
If you need to look up the answers, you will find them in the study guide section.

Answers to the composition questions will vary depending on your
class discussions and the level of your students.

For the vocabulary section of the test, choose ten of the
words from the vocabulary lists to read orally for your students.

The answers to the matching section of the test are below.

Answers to the matching section of the Advanced Short Answer Unit Test
are the same as for Short Answer Unit Test #2.

Test #1	Test #2
1. E	1. J
2. I	2. G
3. H	3. B
4. A	4. F
5. B	5. H
6. J	6. E
7. G	7. I
8. C	8. D
9. F	9. A
10. D	10. C

ADVANCED SHORT ANSWER UNIT TEST - *Inherit the Wind*

I. Matching

___ 1. Melinda　　　　　　　　A. Bailiff

___ 2. Howard　　　　　　　　B. Attorney for the defense

___ 3. Drummond　　　　　　　C. Circuit District Attorney

___ 4. Brady　　　　　　　　　D. Reverend

___ 5. Rachael　　　　　　　　E. Was jailed for teaching about Darwin

___ 6. Cates　　　　　　　　　F. Chief prosecutor in this case

___ 7. Hornbeck　　　　　　　G. Boy exposed to Darwin's ideas

___ 8. Brown　　　　　　　　　H. Brown's daughter

___ 9. Meeker　　　　　　　　I. Reporter from the Baltimore *Herald*

___ 10. Davenport　　　　　　J. Howard called her & her family "worms"

II. Short Answer

1. What issues are on trial in *Inherit the Wind*? Explain using examples from the text.

2. Compare and contrast Drummond and Brady.

Inherit the Wind Advanced Short Answer Unit Test Page 2

3. How did Rachael change during the play?

4. How and why did the crowd's opinions change during the trial? Explain your answer.

5. Explain Mr. Hornbeck's role in the play.

6. Explain Howard's role in the play.

7. What was Rachael's testimony? What effect did it have on the outcome of the trial?

8. Explain why the Radio Man was included in the play.

Inherit the Wind Advanced Short Answer Unit Test Page 3

III. Composition

The *New York World-Telegram and Sun* said of *Inherit the Wind*, "One of the most moving and meaningful plays of our generation. 'A tidal wave of drama.'" Defend that statement using specific examples from the text.

Inherit the Wind Advanced Short Answer Unit Test Page 4

III. Vocabulary

    Write down the vocabulary words you are given. Go back later and use all of those vocabulary words in a composition relating to *Inherit the Wind*.

MULTIPLE CHOICE UNIT TEST 1 - *Inherit the Wind*

I. Matching/Identify

___ 1. Melinda   A. Chief prosecutor in this case

___ 2. Howard   B. Brown's daughter

___ 3. Drummond   C. Reverend

___ 4. Brady   D. Circuit District Attorney

___ 5. Rachael   E. Howard called her & her family "worms"

___ 6. Cates   F. Bailiff

___ 7. Hornbeck   G. Reporter from the Baltimore *Herald*

___ 8. Brown   H. Attorney for the defense

___ 9. Meeker   I. Boy exposed to Darwin's ideas

___ 10. Davenport   J. Was jailed for teaching about Darwin

II. Multiple Choice

1. Bert Cates was in jail because he read a book to his class. What was the book?
    A. He had read *The Communist Manifesto*, by Marx.
    B. He had read the writings of Confucius.
    C. He had read Darwin's *Origin of the Species*.
    D. He had read Freud's *Interpretation of Dreams*.

2. True or False: E. K. Hornbeck is independent but amiable. He has a way with people and gets them to open up easily. He is quick-witted and makes insightful yet friendly jokes.
    A. True
    B. False

3. Which of the following does not describe Matthew Harrison Brady?
    A. He is the attorney prosecuting the case.
    B. He is a former Presidential candidate.
    C. He is a professor at the Harvard School of Law.
    D. He is a famous speaker with a large following.

Inherit the Wind Multiple Choice Unit Test 1 Page 2

4. What warning does Bert give Rachel?
    A. He tells her that she will be ostracized if she associates with him.
    B. He tells her that she should go to a large northern city that has a more liberal attitude.
    C. He tells her that Brady is out to get her, too.
    D. He tells her that if she repeats things he has talked about to her in confidence, he is sure he will be convicted.

5. What does Reverend Brown pray for when Rachael asks him not to damn Bert?
    A. He calls down "the same curse on those who ask grace for this sinner."
    B. He prays for "the wisdom and grace to see the Lord's holy plan."
    C. He prays for "the demons of evil to flee from this innocent child"
    D. He calls "the avenging angels to lift the sinners and carry them away from temptation."

6. Brady reacts to Reverend Brown's comments by repeating the following quote: "...it is possible to be overzealous, to destroy that which you hope to save--so that nothing is left but emptiness. Remember 'He that troubleth his own house...shall inherit the wind." Where does this quote come from?
    A. Ironically, it comes from the *Origin of the Species*.
    B. It comes from Brady's acceptance speech for the Presidency–a speech he never gaive.
    C. It comes from the Book of Proverbs.
    D. It comes from the writings of Thomas Jefferson.

7. What problem did Drummond have with his expert witnesses?
    A. None of them showed up.
    B. The judge ruled that their testimony was not relevant to the case, and he refused to allow them to be questioned.
    C. They were afraid to testify because they had received threats.
    D. The newspaper, which was paying them, and withdrew its financial support.

8. As a last resort, who does Drummond call to the stand?
    A. He calls. Reverend Brown to the stand.
    B. He calls E. K. Hornbeck to the stand.
    C. He calls Brady to the stand.
    D. He calls himself to the stand.

9. What was the jury's verdict?
    A. They found Bert Cates guilty.
    B. They found Bert Cates not guilty.
    C. It was a hung jury.
    D. Bert got off on a technicality.

Inherit the Wind Multiple Choice Unit Test 1 Page 3

10. What happened to Brady?
    A. He collapsed and died.
    B. He went home to his farm and never again appeared in public.
    C. He went to divinity school.
    D. He vowed to take the case to the Supreme Court.

11. Did Bert win or lose?
    A. He won. Even though he was found guilty, his sentence was very light.
    B. He lost. His future in the town is ruined.
    C. He won but felt bad about doing so.
    D. He lost because his wife left him.

12. Drummond says Brady had the same right as Cates. What right is that?
    A. It is the right to be wrong.
    B. It is the right to live as he believes.
    C. It is the right to appeal the case.
    D. It is the right to privacy after the trial's conclusion.

13. What was not on trial in *Inherit the Wind*?
    A. The right to think
    B. The right to speak
    C. The right to be wrong
    D. The freedom of the press

14. Which is not a conflict in *Inherit the Wind*?
    A. Man versus man
    B. Man versus society
    C. Man versus nature
    D. Man versus himself

15. How did Rachael change during the play?
    A. She became more shy and withdrawn.
    B. She became more outspoken--almost to the point of being rude.
    C. She became more independent.
    D. She started out with her life in order and by the end of the trial she was an emotional wreck because all of the things that gave her life meaning and direction were pulled out from under her.

Inherit the Wind Multiple Choice Unit Test 1 Page 4

III. Composition

"He that troubleth his own house shall inherit the wind: and the fool shall be servant to the wise in heart." Explain the relevance of this quotation to the play, *Inherit the Wind*.

Inherit the Wind Multiple Choice Unit Test 1 Page 5

IV. Vocabulary

___ 1. Ominous   a. One who does not believe in god

___ 2. Insinuate   b. Gentle; friendly

___ 3. Pagan   c. Threatening

___ 4. Glib   d. Come together again for a formal purpose

___ 5. Repast   e. Person who holds controversial opinions

___ 6. Pariah   f. Absurd

___ 7. Lamentations   g. Performed with a natural, offhand ease

___ 8. Innocuously   h. Religion not acknowledging the God of Judaism, Christianity, or Islam

___ 9. Agnostic   i. One who believes there can be no proof of God, but does not deny that God may exist

___ 10. Affable   j. Harmlessly

___ 11. Levity   k. Too full of enthusiasm for a cause

___ 12. Overzealous   l. Statements of grief or mourning

___ 13. Orgy   m. Imply

___ 14. Indignantly   n. With an anger aroused by something unjust

___ 15. Preposterous   o. Uncontrolled or immoderate indulgence in an activity

___ 16. Paradoxically   p. Not Christian, Moslem or Jewish

___ 17. Atheist   q. Frivolity; lightness of manner or speech

___ 18. Reconvene   r. Social outcast

___ 19. Heathen   s. As something exhibiting unexplainable or contradictory aspects

___ 20. Heretic   t. Feast

MULTIPLE CHOICE UNIT TEST 2 - *Inherit the Wind*

I. Matching

___ 1. Melinda   A. Bailiff

___ 2. Howard   B. Attorney for the defense

___ 3. Drummond   C. Circuit District Attorney

___ 4. Brady   D. Reverend

___ 5. Rachael   E. Was jailed for teaching about Darwin

___ 6. Cates   F. Chief prosecutor in this case

___ 7. Hornbeck   G. Boy exposed to Darwin's ideas

___ 8. Brown   H. Brown's daughter

___ 9. Meeker   I. Reporter from the Baltimore *Herald*

___ 10. Davenport   J. Howard called her & her family "worms"

II. Multiple Choice

1. Bert Cates was in jail because he read a book to his class. What was the book?
    A. He had read *The Communist Manifesto* by Marx.
    B. He had read the writings of Confucius.
    C. He had read Freud's *Interpretation of Dreams*.
    D. He had read Darwin's *Origin of the Species*.

2. True or False: E. K. Hornbeck is independent but amiable. He has a way with people and gets them to open up easily. He is quick-witted and makes insightful yet friendly jokes.
    A. False
    B. True

3. Which of the following does not describe Matthew Harrison Brady?
    A. He is the attorney prosecuting the case.
    B. He is a professor at the Harvard School of Law.
    C. He is a former Presidential candidate.
    D. He is a famous speaker with a large following.

Inherit the Wind Multiple Choice Unit Test 2 Page 2

4. What warning does Bert give Rachel?
    A. He tells her that if she repeats things he has talked about to her in confidence, he is sure he will be convicted.
    B. He tells her that she should go to a large northern city that has a more liberal attitude.
    C. He tells her that Brady is out to get her, too.
    D. He tells her that she will be ostracized if she associates with him.

5. What does Reverend Brown pray for when Rachael asks him not to damn Bert?
    A. He prays for "the demons of evil to flee from this innocent child."
    B. He prays for "the wisdom and grace to see the Lord's holy plan."
    C. He calls down "the same curse on those who ask grace for this sinner."
    D. He calls down "the avenging angels to lift the sinners and carry them away from temptation."

6. Brady reacts to Reverend Brown's comments by repeating the following quote: "...it is possible to be overzealous, to destroy that which you hope to save--so that nothing is left but emptiness. Remember ..'He that troubleth his own house...shall inherit the wind." Where does this quote come from?
    A. Ironically, it comes from the *Origin of the Species*.
    B. It comes from the Book of Proverbs.
    C. It comes from Brady's acceptance speech for the Presidency–a speech he never gave.
    D. It comes from the writings of Thomas Jefferson.

7. What problem did Drummond have with his expert witnesses?
    A. None of them showed up.
    B. They were afraid to testify because they had received threats.
    C. The judge ruled that their testimony was not relevant to the case, and he refused to allow them to be questioned.
    D. The newspaper, which was paying them, withdrew its financial support.

8. As a last resort, who does Drummond call to the stand?
    A. He calls Reverend Brown to the stand.
    B. He calls Brady to the stand.
    C. He calls E. K. Hornbeck to the stand.
    D. He calls himself to the stand.

9. What was the jury's verdict?
    A. The case was never completed because Brady died.
    B. They found Bert Cates not guilty.
    C. It was a hung jury.
    D. They found Bert Cates guilty.

Inherit the Wind Multiple Choice Unit Test 2 Page 3

10. What happened to Brady?
    A. He went to divinity school.
    B. He went home to his farm and never again appeared in public.
    C. He collapsed and died.
    D. He vowed to take the case to the Supreme Court.

11. Did Bert win or lose?
    A. He lost. The jury came back with a conviction and a stiff sentence.
    B. He lost. His future in the town is ruined..
    C. He won. The jury came back with a unanimous vote for the defense.
    D. He won. Even though he was found guilty, his sentence was very light.

12. Drummond says Brady had the same right as Cates. What right is that?
    A. It is the right to appeal the case.
    B. It is the right to live as he believes.
    C. It is the right to be wrong.
    D. It is the right to privacy after the trial's conclusion.

13. What was not on trial in *Inherit the Wind*?
    A. The freedom of the press
    B. The right to be wrong
    C. The right to speak
    D. The right to think

14. Which is not a conflict in *Inherit the Wind*?
    A. Man versus nature
    B. Man versus society
    C. Man versus man
    D. Man versus himself

15. How did Rachael change during the play?
    A. She started out with her life in order and by the end of the trial she was an emotional wreck because all of the things that gave her life meaning and direction were pulled out from under her.
    B. She became more outspoken--almost to the point of being rude.
    C. She became more withdrawn.
    D. She became more independent.

Inherit the Wind Multiple Choice Unit Test 2 Page 4

III. Composition

Explain the importance of the lawyers in *Inherit the Wind*. Why was it important to the case that these two particular lawyers were representing each side? Would the case have been decided differently if someone not as capable as Drummond had been representing the defense?

Inherit the Wind Multiple Choice Unit Test 2 Page 5

IV. Vocabulary

___ 1. Ponderously   a. Feast

___ 2. Bulwark   b. Too full of enthusiasm for a cause

___ 3. Paradoxically   c. Something serving as a defense

___ 4. Atheist   d. Uncontrolled or immoderate indulgence in an activity

___ 5. Insinuate   e. With an anger aroused by something unjust

___ 6. Overzealous   f. Deceived

___ 7. Orgy   g. Frivolity; lightness of manner or speech

___ 8. Innocuously   h. Eager to do a service for

___ 9. Pariah   i. Lacking in grace; unwieldy from weight or bulk

___ 10. Levity   j. Performed with a natural, offhand ease

___ 11. Deluded   k. Imply

___ 12. Pagan   l. Social outcast

___ 13. Repast   m. Threatening

___ 14. Obliging   n. As something exhibiting unexplainable or contradictory aspects

___ 15. Indeterminate   o. Harmlessly

___ 16. Hypocrite   p. One who says he believes but in actions shows he believes the opposite

___ 17. Reconvene   q. Not precisely established

___ 18. Glib   r. Not Christian, Moslem or Jewish

___ 19. Ominous   s. One who does not believe in God

___ 20. Indignantly   t. Come together again for a formal purpose

ANSWER SHEET - *Inherit the Wind*
Multiple Choice Unit Tests

I. Matching	II. Multiple Choice	IV. Vocabulary
1. ___	1. ___	1. ___
2. ___	2. ___	2. ___
3. ___	3. ___	3. ___
4. ___	4. ___	4. ___
5. ___	5. ___	5. ___
6. ___	6. ___	6. ___
7. ___	7. ___	7. ___
8. ___	8. ___	8. ___
9. ___	9. ___	9. ___
10. ___	10. ___	10. ___
	11. ___	11. ___
	12. ___	12. ___
	13. ___	13. ___
	14. ___	14. ___
	15. ___	15. ___
		16. ___
		17. ___
		18. ___
		19. ___
		20. ___

ANSWER KEY MULTIPLE CHOICE UNIT TESTS – *Inherit the Wind*

Answers to Unit Test 1 are in the left column. Answers to Unit Test 2 are in the right column.

I. Matching	II. Multiple Choice	IV. Vocabulary
1. E J	1. C D	1. C I
2. I G	2. B A	2. M C
3. H B	3. C B	3. P N
4. A F	4. D A	4. G S
5. B H	5. A C	5. T K
6. J E	6. C B	6. R B
7. G I	7. B C	7. L D
8. C D	8. C B	8. J O
9. F A	9. A D	9. I L
10. D C	10. A C	10. B G
	11. A D	11. Q F
	12. A C	12. K R
	13. D A	13. O A
	14. C A	14. N H
	15. C D	15. F Q
		16. S P
		17. A T
		18. D J
		19. H M
		20. E E

UNIT RESOURCE MATERIALS

BULLETIN BOARD IDEAS - *Inherit the Wind*

1. Save one corner of the board for the best of students' *Inherit the Wind* writing assignments.

2. Take one of the word search puzzles from the extra activities section and with a marker copy it over in a large size on the bulletin board. Write the clue words to find to one side. Invite students prior to and after class to find the words and circle them on the bulletin board.

3. Write several of the most significant quotations from the book onto the board on brightly colored paper.

4. Make a bulletin board listing the vocabulary words for this unit. As you complete sections of the novel and discuss the vocabulary for each section, write the definitions on the bulletin board. (If your board is one students face frequently, it will help them learn the words.)

5. Post articles about the controversy between evolution and creation.

6. If you had a production of this play last year, post pictures you took from it. If you did not do a production of it last year, consider doing one this year and having the yearbook staff take pictures for you (so you can use them for a bulletin board next time!)

7. Have students write their favorite "wise sayings" on the board (like "He that troubleth his own house shall inherit the wind.") This also makes a fun introductory activity.

8. Post articles of criticism about the play.

9. Post articles about famous or important trials that have happened in the courthouse in your town.

10. Make a bulletin board about careers in the criminal justice system, careers in journalism, and careers in education.

EXTRA ACTIVITIES - *Inherit the Wind*

One of the difficulties in teaching a novel is that all students don't read at the same speed. One student who likes to read may take the book home and finish it in a day or two. Sometimes a few students finish the in-class assignments early. The problem, then, is finding suitable extra activities for students.

The best thing I've found is to keep a little library in the classroom. For this unit on *Inherit the Wind,* you might check out from the school library other related books and articles about our justice system, careers in education, science, journalism, or the justice system, scientific discoveries about the origins of man, or critical reviews of the play. A copy of Darwin's *Origin* or the transcript from the Scopes trial would also be interesting for some students to look through.

Other things you may keep on hand are puzzles. We have made some relating directly to *Inherit the Wind* for you. Feel free to duplicate them.

Some students may like to draw. You might devise a contest or allow some extra-credit grade for students who draw characters or scenes from *Inherit the Wind.* Note, too, that if the students do not want to keep their drawings you may pick up some extra bulletin board materials this way. If you have a contest and you supply the prize (a CD or something like that perhaps), you could, possibly, make the drawing itself a non-returnable entry fee.

The pages which follow contain games, puzzles and worksheets. The keys, when appropriate, immediately follow the puzzle or worksheet. There are two main groups of activities: one group for the unit; that is, generally relating to the *Inherit the Wind* text, and another group of activities related strictly to the *Inherit the Wind* vocabulary.

Directions for these games, puzzles, and worksheets are self-explanatory. The object here is to provide you with extra materials you may use in any way you choose.

MORE ACTIVITIES - *Inherit the Wind*

1. Have students design a playbill (inside and out) for *Inherit the Wind*

2. Have students design a bulletin board (ready to be put up; not just sketched) for *Inherit the Wind.*

3. Do a complete production of the play and perform it for other students in your school.

4. Have students research careers in science, the criminal justice system, education and/or journalism.

5. Examine Drummond's questioning technique and the logic he uses.

6. Have your students take an informal poll in your community as to how many people believe in the creation theory versus how many people believe in evolution (and how many people believe in neither or both).

7. Use some of the related topics noted earlier for an in-class library as topics for research, written papers or reports or as topics for guest speakers.

8. Have your students do some thinking or logic games or exercises.

9. Have an attorney come in to discuss the Scopes trial and or the trial as depicted in *Inherit the Wind*.

10. Take your class to your local courthouse to see a trial--or at least to see what the trial area looks like.

WORD SEARCH - *Inherit the Wind*

All words in this list are associated with *Inherit the Wind*. The words are placed backwards, forward, diagonally, up and down. The included words are listed below the word searches.

```
D R U M M O N D M E L I N D A Y O Y H C L S S C
D A L X J T F L J E M E S P K S T R H K C E X B
M V N V N W J X R S E N N Q M L R P I V B M E X
Q Y Q C H O P E F U L K H O I L G K W G Z P G J
S B Q N E L V M F H H V E U L X K T B T I N Z N
B Y Y V L R Y X T I E M G R R O H D Q F D N J C
P S J M J M K S L R D A V R J Q C K J J K R R Y
B D M Y V S J L K A K P D G E Z M O Z M C K S X
Q Z Y E F E S V V D P H R L H H D S M K K C Y Y
B J Q T C B L E W P X W L O I W C X F F O Z M Z
S L U K O N N B V T D I R Z P N I A D P O M Y R
W H F R D P E W I W A N G O N H E F E L O R A M
P I O H O W A R D B B R O W N K E S E T A C T R
D K N R Z R E X W E R T Z Z N G R T H N H R J P
F L T D N H S T C A I A T Y A V I I N A E H E W
K B F D N Q M K T S L D D T B J N S E B P C K H
N S W I H J Y X J Q D J S Y S K J L M W J M S V
```

ACT	DAVENPORT	HOWARD	SCENE
BAIL	DIED	INHERIT	SCOPES
BERT	DRUMMOND	JURORS	SIGN
BIBLE	EK	LAWRENCE	STAGE
BRADY	GUILTY	LEE	TEACHER
BROWN	HEADLINES	MEEKER	THINK
CATES	HERALD	MELINDA	TOMMY
COLONEL	HILLSBORO	ORIGIN	WIFE
COMFORT	HOPEFUL	PROPHET	WIND
DANCER	HORNBECK	RACHAEL	WRONG

CROSSWORD - *Inherit the Wind*

CROSSWORD CLUES - *Inherit the Wind*

ACROSS
3. Act division
6. What happened to Brady
8. Play division
9. Chief prosecutor in the case
10. Brady's title
11. The jury's verdict
14. Bert believed church was to ____ people, not frighten them
16. Mr. Cates
18. When Drummond fights, ____ follow.
21. Author Robert E.
22. It tells at once what kind of a community this is
23. Boy exposed to Darwin's ideas
27. 'You murder a ___ it isn't as bad as murdering an old wives' tale.'
28. Reporter for the Baltimore Herald
30. Opposite of lose
31. One often ---- at a door before entering
34. Word that ends a prayer; means 'so be it'
35. Appendage to which one's hand is attached
36. Howard called her and her family worms
37. How Brady wants the Mayor and Reverend to look for the picture
40. Contraction for 'do not'
41. Stebbins boy who was damned because he died before being baptized
42. Brady has the same right as Cates, the right to be _____
43. Entirely
44. Members of the jury
45. What a jury is when it can't come to a verdict
46. Should

DOWN
1. Read Your _____
2. Herald paid it for Bert
3. Place where play is performed
4. Mr. Hornbeck
5. Fifty per cent
7. Golden
9. Reverend
10. Was jailed for teaching about Darwin
12. ____ the Wind
13. Bert's occupation_____
15. Brown's daughter
17. Howard or Brady or Darwin or anyone has the right to
19. Author Jerome
20. Trial to which Inherit the Wind relates
24. Circuit District Attorney
25. Attorney for the defense _____
26. Bailiff
28. Paper for which Hornbeck is a reporter
29. He that troubleth his own house..shall inherit it
32. Drummond is a lawyer who 'has stalked of this land for 40 years.'
33. The town
34. Darwin studied these
38. Darwin's ___ of the Species
39. Brady's nickname; The ___ from Nebraska__
44. Happiness

CROSSWORD ANSWER KEY - *Inherit the Wind*

		B		B	S	C	E	N	E			H		
	D	I	E	D	A	C	T	K			B	R	A	D Y
		B		A	I	A						R	L	
	C	O	L	O	N	E	L	G	U	I	L	T	Y	C O M F O R T
	A	E		C		E	N	E				W		A
	T		B	E	R	T		H	E	A	D	L	I	N E S C
L	E	E		R		H		E	C	A		C		H
	S			S	I	G	N		R	H	W		H O W A R D
		D		M	N		W	I	F	E	R		P	E	A
H	O	R	N	B	E	C	K	W		T	R	E		L	V
E		U		E		W	I	N			K	N	O C K S		E
R		M		K		H	N				C		O		A M E N
A	R	M		M	E	L	I	N	D A		H	O P E F U L		N		P
L		O		R		L		P		R			R		I		O
D	O	N	T		L			R	I			T O M M Y		R
		D			S	W	R	O	N G		R		A		T
				B		P		I		T	O T A L L Y	
		J	U	R O R S		H U N G		O		S	
		O		R		E				M		
		Y		O	U	G	H	T		S		

MATCHING QUIZ/WORKSHEET 1 - *Inherit the Wind*

___ 1. HILLSBORO   A. Reverend

___ 2. HERALD   B. Brady has the same right as Cates, the right to be_____

___ 3. BAIL   C. Author Jerome

___ 4. HEADLINES   D. Paper for which Hornbeck is a reporter

___ 5. PROPHET   E. Stebbins boy who was damned because he died before being baptized

___ 6. WRONG   F. Howard called her and her family worms

___ 7. DANCER   G. The jury's verdict

___ 8. COMFORT   H. The town

___ 9. EK   I. Boy exposed to Darwin's ideas

___ 10. SCENE   J. Bert believed church was to ____ people, not frighten them

___ 11. CATES   K. Brady's nickname; The ___ from Nebraska

___ 12. DIED   L. When Drummond fights, ____ follow.

___ 13. MELINDA   M. Reporter for the Baltimore *Herald*

___ 14. SIGN   N. What happened to Brady

___ 15. GUILTY   O. It tells at once what kind of a community this is

___ 16. TOMMY   P. Act division

___ 17. BROWN   Q. Was jailed for teaching about Darwin

___ 18. HOWARD   R. Mr. Hornbeck

___ 19. LAWRENCE   S. Herald paid it for Bert

___ 20. HORNBECK   T. Golden _____

MATCHING QUIZ/WORKSHEET 2 - *Inherit the Wind*

___ 1. ACT   A. Bert's occupation

___ 2. TEACHER   B. Stebbins boy who was damned because he died before being baptized

___ 3. SIGN   C. Brady has the same right as Cates, the right to be _____

___ 4. TOMMY   D. Was jailed for teaching about Darwin

___ 5. LEE   E. He that troubleth his own house..shall inherit it

___ 6. HOPEFUL   F. Play division

___ 7. WRONG   G. Herald paid it for Bert

___ 8. HILLSBORO   H. What happened to Brady

___ 9. HERALD   I. Boy exposed to Darwin's ideas

___ 10. BAIL   J. Act division

___ 11. HOWARD   K. The town

___ 12. WIND   L. Members of the jury

___ 13. BROWN   M. How Brady wants the Mayor and Reverend to look for the picture

___ 14. SCENE   N. It tells at once what kind of a community this is

___ 15. CATES   O. Reverend

___ 16. DIED   P. Chief prosecutor in the case

___ 17. MELINDA   Q. Paper for which Hornbeck is a reporter

___ 18. JURORS   R. Bert believed church was to ____ people, not frighten them

___ 19. COMFORT   S. Howard called her and her family worms

___ 20. BRADY   T. Author Robert E.

KEY: MATCHING QUIZ/WORKSHEETS - *Inherit the Wind*

Worksheet 1	Worksheet 2
1. H	1. F
2. D	2. A
3. S	3. N
4. L	4. B
5. K	5. T
6. B	6. M
7. T	7. C
8. J	8. K
9. R	9. Q
10. P	10. G
11. Q	11. I
12. N	12. E
13. F	13. O
14. O	14. J
15. G	15. D
16. E	16. H
17. A	17. S
18. I	18. L
19. C	19. R
20. M	20. P

JUGGLE LETTER REVIEW GAME CLUE SHEET - *Inherit the Wind*

SCRAMBLED	WORD	CLUE
CKHBRNOE	HORNBECK	Reporter to the Baltimore *Herald*
YGLIUT	GUILTY	The jury's verdict
MDRUDNMO	DRUMMOND	Attorney for the defense
DDIE	DIED	What happened to Brady
RDLEAH	HERALD	Paper for which Hornbeck is a reporter
ONRBW	BROWN	Reverend
INDW	WIND	He that troubleth his own house...shall inherit it
EWIF	WIFE	'You murder a _____ it isn't as bad as murdering an old wives' tale.'
REIHITN	INHERIT	_____ the Wind
TAC	ACT	Play division
ILBROOSHL	HILLSBORO	The town
ELE	LEE	Author Robert E.
LIBA	BAIL	Herald paid it for Bert
PDARTONEV	DAVENPORT	Circuit District Attorney
EEERKM	MEEKER	Bailiff
ISNG	SIGN	It tells at once what kind of a community this is
ONLEOCL	COLONEL	Brady's title
PEUHLOF	HOPEFUL	How Brady wants the Mayor and Reverend to look for the picture
BBLEI	BIBLE	Read Your _____
TEROPHP	PROPHET	Brady's nickname; the _____ from Nebraska
GNROW	WRONG	Brady has the same right as Cates, the right to be __
TESCA	CATES	Was jailed for teaching about Darwin
YMTOM	TOMMY	Stebbins boys who was damned because he died before being baptized
ASETG	STAGE	Place where play is performed
DBYRA	BRADY	Chief prosecutor in the case
NHILESDALE	HEADLINES	When Drummond fights, _____ follow
EOSSCP	SCOPES	Trial to which Inherit the Wind relates
RTOCMFO	COMFORT	Bert believed church was to _____ people, not to frighten them
MOSROUROTC	COURTROOMS	Drummond is a lawyer who 'has stalked _____ of this land for 40 years.
KE	EK	Mr. Hornbeck
ALACERH	RACHAEL	Brown's daughter
LIADMEN	MELINDA	Howard called her and her family worms
NEESC	SCENE	Act division

VOCABULARY RESOURCE MATERIALS

VOCABULARY WORD SEARCH - *Inherit the Wind*

All words in this list are associated with *Inherit the Wind* with an emphasis on the vocabulary words chosen for study in the text. The words are placed backwards, forward, diagonally, up and down. The included words are listed below.

```
F S V L A Q W X C P F C C R T P Z Z D W Q M Y Y
D C U P A G A N E H T A E H K R A W L U B R G V
K P L O T N R W T Y P F T S H E R J Z Z R P T
N S R I N T T O X L A O E F A D Y C I L O X N Y
X Y B A Q I C Y S S I R M R A U A P O A C R T B
F S L D N I M U T T U N T I D B N T O N H I Y B
Y G G E T I O O I I I O D S S I L I H C V K W L
W P N E V R M D V N N C R E O S T E S E R E P D
D T R I E I S O E E N D N E T R I I L N I I N P
D E N D G F T R S L R O I Q T E P O O R I S T E
H V N V P I C A C I U Z C G C S R B N N C W T E
P O V Z K R L H T B T D E U N Z O M Q X J F M Y
P J W L N Y H B C N B Y E A O A C P I F K B F K
F Z W V N K G K O D E N W D L U N R E N X B T F
B P H B N B N C D J J T P D J O S T P R A P F R
C M R R R C X D T M H Q L K P K U L L K P T Z Y
Z K F N L X D N S L P Y C N W F H S Y Y M Y E V
```

AFFABLE	HERETIC	OMINOUS	PONDEROUSLY
AGNOSTIC	HYPOCRITE	OMISSION	PREPOSTEROUS
ANIMOSITY	INDETERMINATE	ORGY	PROSTRATE
ATHEIST	INDIGNANTLY	OVERZEALOUS	RECONVENE
BULWARK	INNOCUOUSLY	PAGAN	REPAST
DELUDED	INSINUATE	PARIAH	TENTATIVELY
GLIB	LEVITY	PERDITION	HEATHEN
	OBLIGING	PERTINENT	

VOCABULARY CROSSWORD - *Inherit the Wind*

VOCABULARY CROSSWORD CLUES - *Inherit the Wind*

ACROSS
1. Religion not acknowledging the God of Judaism, Christianity, or Islam
4. Absurd
10. Social outcast
11. One who does not believe in God
15. Not Christian, Moslem or Jewish
16. Insert
18. With an anger aroused by something unjust
19. Reverend
20. Something serving as a defense
23. Short, affirmative head gesture
25. A single
26. Prefix meaning three
27. Not precisely established
29. Allow
30. Darwin's ___ of the Species
31. What happened to Brady
34. Lying flat
36. Stebbins boy who was damned because he died before being baptized
39. Was jailed for teaching about Darwin
41. The judge ---- against most of Drummond's motions
42. That which relates to the matter at hand
45. Eager to do a service for
49. Something that is left out
50. Look
51. Negative reply
52. Howard or Brady or Darwin or anyone has the right to _____
53. Gentle; friendly

DOWN
2. Mr. Hornbeck
3. Person who holds controversial opinions
5. Feast
6. Come together again for a formal purpose
7. Play division
8. One who says he believes but in actions shows he believes the opposite
9. Uncontrolled or immoderate indulgence in an activity
11. Bitter hostility or hatred
12. A bad offense against God
13. As something exhibiting unexplainable or contradictory aspects
14. Deceived
17. Act division
19. Herald paid it for Bert
20. Cause to reproduce in a selected manner
21. Statements of grief or mourning
22. One who believes there can be no proof of God, but does not deny that God may exist
24. Frivolity; lightness of manner or speech
28. Members of the newspaper media; also machine that prints newspapers
32. If something is a fact, it is ----
33. Eternal damnation
35. How Brady wants the Mayor and Reverend to look for the picture
37. Threatening
38. Chief prosecutor in the case
40. Evidence is labeled with these
43. Darwin gave one theory about how mankind came to ----; be
44. It tells at once what kind of a community this is
46. Author Robert E.
47. Performed with a natural, offhand ease
48. 'You murder a ___ it isn't as bad as murdering an old wives' tale.'

VOCABULARY CROSSWORD - *Inherit the Wind*

VOCABULARY WORKSHEET 1 - *Inherit the Wind*

___ 1. OMINOUS   A. One who does not believe in God

___ 2. INSINUATE   B. Gentle; friendly

___ 3. PAGAN   C. Threatening

___ 4. GLIB   D. Come together again for a formal purpose

___ 5. REPAST   E. Person who holds controversial opinions

___ 6. PARIAH   F. Absurd

___ 7. LAMENTATIONS   G. Performed with a natural, offhand ease

___ 8. INNOCUOUSLY   H. Religion not acknowledging the God of Judaism, Christianity, or Islam

___ 9. AGNOSTIC   I. One who believes there can be no proof of God, but does not deny that God may exist

___ 10. AFFABLE   J. Harmlessly

___ 11. LEVITY   K. Too full of enthusiasm for a cause

___ 12. OVERZEALOUS   L. Statements of grief or mourning

___ 13. ORGY   M. Imply

___ 14. INDIGNANTLY   N. With an anger aroused by something unjust

___ 15. PREPOSTEROUS   O. Uncontrolled or immoderate indulgence in an activity

___ 16. PARADOXICALLY   P. Not Christian, Moslem or Jewish

___ 17. ATHEIST   Q. Frivolity; lightness of manner or speech

___ 18. RECONVENE   R. Social outcast

___ 19. HEATHEN   S. As something exhibiting unexplainable or contradictory aspects

___ 20. HERETIC   T. Feast

VOCABULARY WORKSHEET 2 - *Inherit the Wind*

___ 1. Not Christian, Moslem or Jewish
      a. Pagan   b. Reconvene   c. Deluded   d. Orgy

___ 2. One who believes there can be no proof of God, but does not deny that God may exist
      a. Pagan   b. Omission   c. Insinuate   d. Agnostic

___ 3. Deceived
      a. Indeterminate   b. Pariah   c. Heretic   d. Deluded

___ 4. That which relates to the matter at hand
      a. Pertinent   b. Agnostic   c. Paradoxically   d. Orgy

___ 5. With an anger aroused by something unjust
      a. Indignantly   b. Reconvene   c. Repast   d. Levity

___ 6. Eager to do a service for
      a. Levity   b. Obliging   c. Atheist   d. Affable

___ 7. Too full of enthusiasm for a cause
      a. Repast   b. Overzealous   c. Lamentations   d. Reconvene

___ 8. Something serving as a defense
      a. Agnostic   b. Tentatively   c. Overzealous   d. Bulwark

___ 9. Imply
      a. Ponderously   b. Hypocrite   c. Insinuate   d. Agnostic

___ 10. Social outcast
      a. Pariah   b. Agnostic   c. Overzealous   d. Indignantly

___ 11. Statements of grief or mourning
      a. Indignantly   b. Ominous   c. Lamentations   d. Prostrate

___ 12. As something exhibiting unexplainable or contradictory aspects
      a. Orgy   b. Paradoxically   c. Heretic   d. Obliging

___ 13. Harmlessly
      a. Heretic   b. Insinuate   c. Innocuously   d. Hypocrite

___ 14. Come together again for a formal purpose
      a. Indignantly   b. Pertinent   c. Reconvene   d. Ponderously

___ 15. Feast
      a. Pagan   b. Repast   c. Pertinent   d. Prostrate

___ 16. Hesitantly; uncertainly
      a. Innocuously   b. Heretic   c. Ponderously   d. Tentatively

___ 17. Bitter hostility or hatred
      a. Animosity   b. Heathen   c. Deluded   d. Lamentations

___ 18. Something that is left out
      a. Repast   b. Omission   c. Hypocrite   d. Insinuate

___ 19. Uncontrolled or immoderate indulgence in an activity
      a. Orgy   b. Pertinent   c. Pariah   d. Heretic

___ 20. Lacking in grace; unwieldy from weight or bulk
      a. Ponderously   b. Omission   c. Deluded   d. Levity

KEY: VOCABULARY WORKSHEETS - *Inherit the Wind*

Worksheet 1	Worksheet 2
1. C	1. A
2. M	2. D
3. P	3. D
4. G	4. A
5. T	5. A
6. R	6. B
7. L	7. B
8. J	8. D
9. I	9. C
10. B	10. A
11. Q	11. C
12. K	12. B
13. O	13. C
14. N	14. C
15. F	15. B
16. S	16. D
17. A	17. A
18. D	18. B
19. H	19. A
20. E	20. A

VOCABULARY JUGGLE LETTER REVIEW GAME CLUES - *Inherit the Wind*

SCRAMBLED	WORD	CLUE
RAKLBWU	BULWARK	Something serving as a defense
TIEINORPD	PERDITION	Eternal damnation
OUORSPLEYND	PONDEROUSLY	Lacking in grace; unwieldy from weight or bulk
ONSTGACI	AGNOSTIC	One who believes there can be no proof of God, but does not deny that God may exist
NYCNLOIOUSU	INNOCUOUSLY	Harmlessly
NAAGP	PAGAN	Not Christian, Moslem or Jewish
LIBG	GLIB	Performed with a natural, offhand ease
NTPEERNTI	PERTINENT	That which relates to the matter at hand
SIUOMNO	OMINOUS	Threatening
RGYO	ORGY	Uncontrolled or immoderate indulgence in an activity
EICTHER	HERETIC	Person who holds controversial opinions
YVLITAEETNT	TENTATIVELY	Hesitantly; uncertainly
TTSAHIE	ATHEIST	One who does not believe in God
EZULAOROESV	OVERZEALOUS	Too full of enthusiasm for a cause
IVEYLT	LEVITY	Frivolity; lightness of manner or speech
SEPRARTOT	PROSTRATE	Lying flat
EAUTSIINN	INSINUATE	Imply
LGONIGIB	OBLIGING	Eager to do a service for
ESTRPA	REPAST	Feast
TPYHEIOCR	HYPOCRITE	One who says he believes but in actions shows he believes the opposite
MOATIIYNS	ANIMOSITY	Bitter hostility or hatred
EROOPUESTPSR	PREPOSTEROUS	Absurd
ISTNTNEAOMLA	LAMENTATIONS	Statements of grief or mourning
EDDLUDE	DELUDED	Deceived
LYGNDTNNIAI	INDIGNANTLY	With an anger aroused by something unjust
MNSIOSOI	OMISSION	Something that is left out
NREECNVEO	RECONVENE	Come together again for a formal purpose
NAEEHHT	HEATHEN	Religion not acknowledging the God of Judaism, Christianity or Islam
AFFBLEA	AFFABLE	Gentle; friendly
SPAETR	REPAST	Feast
AAPRHI	PARIAH	Social outcast

www.ingramcontent.com/pod-product-compliance
Lightning Source LLC
Chambersburg PA
CBHW051418070526
44584CB00023B/3488